DELIVERING QUALITY IN VOCATIONAL EDUCATION

NEW DEVELOPMENTS IN VOCATIONAL EDUCATION

Series Editors: Peter Funnell and Dave Müller

DELIVERING QUALITY IN VOCATIONAL EDUCATION

DAVE MÜLLER
PETER FUNNELL

KOGAN PAGE

To Vik, Emily and Lucy
Sue, Simon and Rebecca
for being there and being patient

First published in 1991

Kogan Page Limited
120 Pentonville Road
London N1 9JN

British Library Cataloguing in Publication Data
A CIP record for this book is available from the British Library.
ISBN 0 74940 174 5

Typeset by DP Photosetting, Aylesbury, Bucks
Printed and bound in Great Britain by
Clays Ltd, St Ives plc

Contents

Acknowledgements

In preparation of this book thanks are due to Joe Byrne and Chris Parker of Suffolk College for their help and to Dolores Black of Kogan Page for her interest.

Series Preface

Currently enjoying renewed interest, vocational education has experienced substantial change during recent years in terms of its curriculum delivery and organization. It has faced up to the implications of the demographic downturn and is now responding positively to the challenge of the Single European Market and wider structural changes within Europe. The responsibility for vocational education is now shared more widely within the government between the Department of Education and Science and the Department of Employment. Changing government policy and practice during the 1980s has created an environment which is more competitive both between public sector institutions and private education and training providers.

The recognition that the United Kingdom has failed by European standards to provide sufficient training to meet employer needs has led to policies which aim to increase the participation rate for those aged 16 and over. The 1990s will witness the continuation and heightening of this process of change and the generation of new opportunities and challenges for those responsible for providing vocational education.

This series will focus on these opportunities and challenges. The aim will be to provide contemporary texts which focus on newly emerging issues in vocational education, with an emphasis on innovation. More specifically the series will seek to influence and inform practice by focusing on the application of new and original ideas. In this way the texts will be at the interface between theory and practice with the explicit intention of enabling practitioners and managers to apply new educational ideas and philosophies.

The books are designed for those engaged professionally in vocational education and will provide information on, and critical analyses of, new developments. The contemporary and applied nature of the series will furnish a valuable source of material on important current issues and will build into a library to illustrate the application of good practice. We hope you enjoy this and other texts in the series.

Peter Funnell and Dave Müller
Ipswich 1991

Foreword

The bringing together of a number of perspectives on quality in vocational education in a single volume is both welcome and timely. It is welcome because it adds to the limited literature on both vocational education and the concept of quality in education and training. It is timely because vocational education is now a centre-stage issue not only in secondary, further and higher education but also in the industrial and business sector.

This prominence is evidenced by, for example, the formalization of vocational education in schools through the Technical Vocational Education Initiative and BTEC First Diplomas; the massive curriculum development taking place in 16–19 education, particularly in relationship to the National Council for Vocational Qualifications; the increased emphasis on vocational courses in higher education as the system accommodates more eligible students; and the greater involvement of employers in vocational education and training through contact with schools and through the Training Enterprise Councils and the Training Credit Pilot Schemes.

It is also timely in relation to the growing interest in quality in education and training. The motivation behind such interest can come from those responsible for funding in the accelerating drive to establish value for money, or the increasing interest of clients in the relationship between education and training and the world of work, or educational providers who wish to see students emerging not just with knowledge and competences of immediate use but with attitudes and skills which will serve them well in the future.

The contributions within this book address the issue of quality in vocational education from various standpoints. Part 1 is introductory and explores the concept of quality in relationship to vocational education. Part 2 focuses on quality in the context of students as clients. It considers student learning, concepts of core skills and independent study. Part 3 introduces the perspective of employer as client. It features the role of the newly established Training Enterprise Councils and presents two case studies, one on consultancy and the other on enterprise. Part 4 has as its theme product and system quality control while Part 5 brings together a number of the major themes within the book and seeks a way forward.

Overall, the book has a student-centred approach with an emphasis on models of learning, rather than of teaching. The notion that students should be major stakeholders in creating and evaluating the product is particularly significant. Given the low participation rate in our training systems compared with the rates of our major competitors, any development which gives emphasis to individual client motivation and aspiration in the context of quality vocational education is to be warmly welcomed.

This book makes a major contribution to the debate about quality issues within post-school vocational education and training. It should be of interest to all concerned in that field, whether provider or consumer.

Derek Mortimer, OBE
Principal, Suffolk College

List of Contributors

Barbara Aitken	Lecturer in Business Studies, Suffolk College, Ipswich
Ronald Barnett	Centre for Higher Education, Institute of Education, University of London
Tony Barry	Director, Consultancy and Development Unit, Cardiff Institute of Higher Education
Mike Bax	Managing Director, Suffolk Training and Enterprise Council
Peter Funnell	Head of Creative Studies, Suffolk College, Ipswich
Sarah Guri	Everyman's University, Israel
David Hind	Department of Marketing and Tourism Management, Newcastle Upon Tyne Polytechnic
Eunice Hinds	Head of School for Independent Study, Polytechnic of East London
David Lilley	Director, Suffolk Management Development Centre
Derek Mortimer	Principal, Suffolk College, Ipswich
Charles Muir	Consortium Development Co-ordinator 16 to 19, Suffolk LEA, Bury St Edmunds
Dave Müller	Vice-Principal, Suffolk College, Ipswich
Keith Norris	Head of Faculty of Technology, Suffolk College, Ipswich
Geoff Stanton	Head of the Further Education Unit, London
Sharron Wardman-Browne	Lecturer in Office Skills, Suffolk College
Mantz Yorke	Assistant Rector and Director of Institutional Audit, The Liverpool Polytechnic

PART I

Introductory Perspectives

1 Delivering Quality: A Managerial and an Industrial Perspective

During the 1980s an increasing commitment emerged in the commercial and industrial sector to developing and delivering 'quality'. This movement has been typified by the pioneering work of individuals such as Crosby (1978; 1989) Peters and Waterman (1982) and Deming (1988). These and other contributors to the quality debate have been perceived as having influenced the introduction of 'Total Quality Management' (TQM) for a wide range of manufacturing industries, and in particular in countries such as Japan. Japanese manufacturers are often held up as prime examples of organizations which have fully embraced the 'quality revolution' and in doing so have made themselves infinitely more successful and competitive than their Western counterparts.

More recently the West has placed a greater emphasis on the search for excellence, having initially rejected the quality movement as being too radical and lacking demonstrable benefits (Oakland, 1989a). This is no longer the case, and in order to remain competitive, Western managers, and in particular those in the USA and the UK, are seeking to implement TQM procedures into both manufacturing and service industries. This movement is having a significant impact, not only on private, but also on public sector institutions, both of which are now becoming far more in tune with the market place.

Defining quality

What then is the 'quality movement' committed to and how is the concept of 'quality' operationalized? At a simple level, *delivering quality requires understanding and conforming to customers' requirements and needs*. In this sense, quality is conforming to customer requirements, whether the customer be external to the organization or in-house as part of the production process. Implicit in this process is *getting it right first time*, which implies that there are no errors or mistakes in the end product. This is often referred to in the literature as *zero defect*. In practice this means that quality is built into the process rather than using a procedure in which deficient products are inspected out. It is not the product which is subject to quality control, but the production process itself, the aim being to ensure that the end product conforms to customer requirements. Those organizations which cannot develop and produce what the customer requires, and in doing so overcome the technological and personal obstacles, are unlikely to survive through the 1990s.

The key to success in introducing a quality approach is to put in place management systems which in themselves are committed to the delivery of total quality. TQM at a minimum level can only function effectively on the basis of having determined exactly what the customer requires. The need for sophisticated market research is paramount in delivering quality. Having determined what the customer requires, it is then necessary to evaluate the extent to which the existing procedures and systems set up to deliver the product or service are effective. The twist here is that efficient and technologically advanced systems of producing manufacturing goods or services are not in themselves of value, unless they contribute to meeting customer specifications. At the same time it has to be recognized that within any production process there are both external customers who need the final product or service, and internal customers who are part of the production process. Internal customers rely on each other in order to satisfy external demand and therefore require the same adherence to excellence as those purchasing or receiving the product or service. From a managerial perspective this requires establishing a common goal towards delivering quality at all levels of any production process. Finally, in striving for quality it is necessary to be able to measure the extent to which the processes conform to the requirements of internal and external customers.

This process is perhaps best summed up by Price (1984) in his very practical text on delivering quality in manufacturing industries. Price notes that there are four simple questions to pose and find answers to:

- Can you make it OK?
- Are we making it OK?
- Have we made it OK?
- Could we make it better?

Having first determined what the customer requires, these questions help the manufacturer or the deliverer of the service to focus on precise objectives when reviewing existing procedures. There is no mileage in trying to conform to customer requirements if the product or service cannot in the first instance be delivered. It is also important to ensure that the production or delivery process facilitates a 'zero defect' product. It is then necessary to see to what extent the product conforms to customer specifications. Finally one has to ensure that the demands of the most exacting customers are met and there should be a continual process of striving to upgrade quality beyond mere conformity to customer requirements. Marketing is as much a part of creating a customer specification as defining it.

In general, then, quality is customer-driven and is the total of all those things which combine to satisfy the needs of the market place. This results in customers demanding more and continuing to purchase the product or service because there is no imbalance between quality, cost and availability (Milner, 1990). In order to attain this level of competitiveness, organizations have to be managed in such a way as to ensure customer satisfaction at every stage of the manufacturing or service process, both for internal and external customers. TQM is the procedure by which organizations are structured so that customer expectations are met, and in which the potential to exceed the demands of customers is always present.

Objectives of 'Total Quality Management'

The single and overriding aim of the emphasis on quality and the introduction of appropriate management systems is quite simply to enhance and improve profitability. It is the bottom line which drives managerial innovation and provides the evidence to support major changes in the ways in which manufacturing and servicing industries function. It is, however, important to recognize that in order to become profitable, the total quality approach places specific emphasis on attaining the highest possible level of customer satisfaction. By focusing directly on the needs of customers and putting their interests first, profitability is maintained and enhanced through increased competitiveness. The end product of meeting customer needs and introducing quality systems is indeed to become more competitive and to gain a larger and more profitable share of the market.

A case study by Harvey (1989) reviews the development of a TQM strategy for a large, diverse engineering and manufacturing Company. As part of the implementation process the Company identified eight strategic objectives:

- to improve attention to the customer;
- to improve business reliability and operating efficiency;
- to improve investment in people;
- to improve housekeeping and orderliness;
- to deliver high quality products and services – defect free;

- to improve employee communications;
- to establish clearer departmental goals;
- to facilitate a more open style of management and team building (p 33).

The Company's commitment to these objectives was seen as essential in achieving improved competitiveness and enhanced customer service.

However, in themselves the strategic objectives do not relate specifically to profit, but focus on the needs of customers, the development of procedures to improve operations and a more open and communicative style of management. For this to work successfully employees need to embrace the customer perspective and to take responsibility for initiating and revising existing procedures in line with this. Therefore, the major thrust of becoming more profitable and customer centred is to focus on those people responsible for the production process or service delivery. As Crosby (1989) has emphasized, it is not until managers are prepared to take responsibility themselves for the problems they have created for others, that clear strategic objectives can be agreed and implemented.

It remains, however, relatively simple to identify the outcomes of successful quality management. Given that above all it includes increased profitability, the benefits linked directly to this include:

- a higher level of commitment to quality by management;
- greater awareness of quality by the workforce;
- the elimination of waste;
- greater emphasis on prevention;
- greater use of working together in teams;
- more defect-free products or services;
- greater identification with the customer, whether external or internal;
- the introduction of agreed working procedures;
- the creation of an organizational culture in which quality is emphasized.

Harvey (1989) and others list similar features as immediate benefits which accrue from introducing TQM.

BS 5750/ISO 9000: national and international standards for quality systems

The implementation of TQM requires that clear procedures for maintaining quality be laid down and adhered to. Consequently there is the need to apply a set of agreed standards which have external credibility. The introduction of the British Standard 5750 in 1979 was a means of specifying the features of an organization's quality assurance system. It is based on the assumption that for all stages of production from the initial contract to the finished product, there will be clear statements governing those aspects of quality which should be identifiable and how they will be assessed. To be seen to comply with the requirements of BS 5750, it is necessary for the organization to be audited by a third party and registered by the British Standards Institution. More recently there has been a much wider interest in quality standards which has led to the International Organization for Standardization completing its work and producing ISO 9000 which is based on, and derived mainly from, BS 5750.

Once Companies obtain registration, it is anticipated that there will be a significant chain reaction on their suppliers to ensure they meet the same quality standards. It is the independent assessment by an accredited certification body that provides the assurance that certain quality standards are being met and in the long term contribute to greater profitability. The procedures are likely to be more efficient and accreditation demonstrates to customers the commitment to quality as well as signalling the ability to supply an appropriate product or service. Customers are beginning to specify that the quality of goods and services they wish to purchase should be controlled by management systems complying with BS 5750, and this in itself has been a very powerful motivator for gaining accreditation.

In setting up a quality system it is necessary to document carefully all those procedures and processes which lead to the development of the product or service in such a way that clear responsibilities are laid down, and no employee is unclear about his or her own contribution and the procedures which should be followed. The quality system includes customer liaison, the manufacturing and purchasing processes, detailed information on sub-contracting and a significant emphasis on staff training. These controls are made explicit in a guide produced by the British Standards Institution, and published by the Department of Trade and Industry:

> In a logical sequence you will need to establish and control the functions of design and development planning, assigning activities to qualified staff with adequate resources, controlling interfaces between different disciplines and organizations, documenting design input requirements and documenting design output in terms of requirements and calculations.
>
> You will need to assign competent personnel to verify that the design output meets the design input requirement and operate documented procedures to control all design changes and modifications. Careful, planned and documented control at each stage – as per BS 5750 – is commonsense business practice, ensures a smooth passage from drawing board to end product and ensures that products are designed safe for use (p 9).

The essence of this approach is to ensure that the manufacturing or service process is clearly documented and that there are clear work instructions to cover every phase of the manufacture, development, assembly and installation process. What is needed then in many manufacturing and service industries is the production of 'Quality Manuals'.

The use of ISO 9000 is compatible with the introduction of a TQM approach. A major component of this approach is making explicit the methods by which a management system incorporates all the activities associated with quality. As Oakland (1989a) points out, ISO 9000 encourages manufacturing and service industries to set out the methods by which a management system can be implemented so that all the specified performance requirements and needs of the customer are fully met. Similarly, Harvey (1989) implemented total quality alongside the introduction of a Company-wide quality assurance strategy based on ISO 9000. This resulted in a series of 'Total Quality Management Policy Quality Assurance Documentation' covering all the procedures relating to the production process.

However, the emphasis on documenting procedures is not in itself the introduction of a total quality approach. Inherent in ISO 9000 is the danger that the documentation will take over the process and that the organization will become committed not to quality management, but to the production of quality documentation. Whereas ISO 9000 does provide an external seal of approval and can readily be incorporated as part of a total quality approach, it only facilitates changes in procedures not people. Nor is it as responsive in terms of meeting the needs of customers, as the procedures in themselves may be given priority over the identified needs of customers. There is familiarity and comfort in having a laid-down set of procedures such as those which determine Income Tax or Social Security claims, and at times it is difficult to break through such well-structured documentation in order to impose a customer perspective of quality on the process. With these limitations in mind, ISO 9000 can be used alongside the introduction of a TQM approach, or as a useful tool with which to influence quality procedures within an organization. As such, and until total quality procedures themselves are accredited in their own right, there will be a role for the International Standards Organization to play in formally certifying quality assurance procedures, especially for manufacturing industries, and maybe in the future for service industries such as education.

Implementing Total Quality Management

The introduction of TQM needs to be undertaken systematically and emphasis must be placed on management commitment and employee involvement. Oakland (1989a) has set out in detail a series of steps to help management develop total quality procedures. Figure 1.1 is derived from his book. He expands on these steps in his more recent book, *Total Quality Management* (1989b). The steps begin with the development of an organizational commitment, and hence a clear policy position on quality, and lead on to the design and implementation stage, ensuring at all times management support through action, not statements. It is interesting to note the introduction of training at what might be seen as a late stage in the model. Training is, however, critical in ensuring successful implementation. In terms of specifying ISO 9000, this would happen at the middle stage in developing a system. The importance of structuring the introduction of TQM does ensure that those involved cover the critical steps in a more or less logical order, and creates institutional and employee commitment.

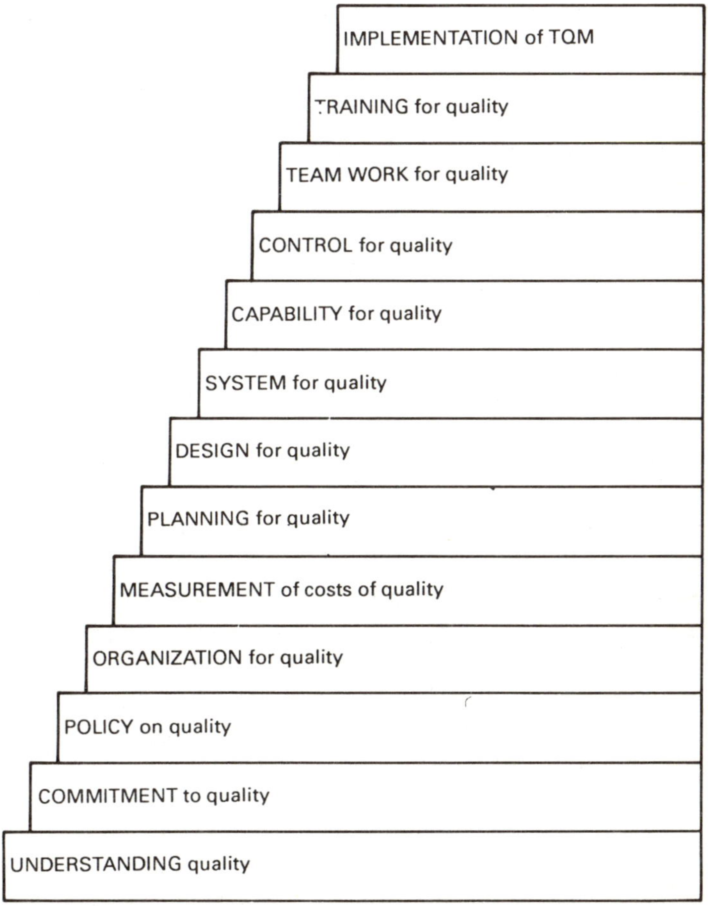

Figure 1.1 *The Steps to TQM* (Oakland, 1989a)

Crosby (1989), in a more colloquial style, has developed what he refers to as a 14-step process in implementing the philosophy of quality. He starts with the development of management commitment and the establishment of a quality improvement team to undertake a series of quality measures. This, he suggests, leads to establishing the extent to which the lack of quality is expensive. This, he argues, creates the need to establish quality awareness and the undertaking of corrective actions with a view to producing zero defect products or services. At this stage Crosby introduces considerable employee education and seeks commitment to quality and the establishment of specific goals. This assists in removing errors which he believes should be recognized through simple procedures such as saying 'thank you' and to the formal establishment of 'Quality Councils' which are responsible for an organization's 'wellness'. Finally, he argues, step 14 is to do it again! These steps he sees as guidelines, not instructions, but above all he emphasizes the need for involvement, commitment and action. There is little, if any, gain in laying out formal procedures unless individuals are given the scope to take responsibility for innovating quality management. External standards and procedures in their own right do not lead to the delivery of quality but are contributory factors. It is the entrepreneurial skills of individuals and their ability to lead which is the main contributing factor.

Involvement in developing total quality

In implementing a TQM system it is essential that managers recognize the potential impact such an approach may have on the total organization. It is critical that each and every employee in the organization becomes actively involved in the total quality process. Employees must be given ownership of the issue and responsibility within which they can act. This involves a significant change in the attitudes of many, if not all, employees. The challenge lies not in changing the organization but in enabling people to develop and change themselves (Oakland 1989a). The Company is the sum of those involved in it, and therefore change cannot be external to the main players. This poses significant opportunities to enhance staff training and development and for senior management to show a commitment on behalf of the organization to resourcing the re-education of employees and themselves.

From an organizational perspective there will result a new framework within which decisions are made. Successful organizations will take full account of the needs of their customers, while including their own suppliers as part of the total quality package. The organization will have a much-changed philosophy which is more outward looking and seeks to influence the behaviour and performance of others. Hence, in such an organization significant stress must be placed on making marketing as well as quality a major focus of any implementation strategy. This in itself entails developing effective communication within the organization and fostering team work and team building in order that the corporate aim of the organization can be assimilated by employees as part of their everyday working philosophy. It is through the empowering of individuals that organizations change; but it is through the leadership qualities of individuals that the culture for change is created. Delivering quality entails a radical and positive review of an organization's internal structures and external focus. This in turn involves those individuals directly responsible for creating the culture: that is, the complete workforce.

'Total Quality Management' and beyond: What then of the future?

Of some significance to the quality movement is Peters'(1988) recent thesis, *Thriving on Chaos*. He argues that managers, and hence organizations, must learn to live with and love change. He is unconvinced of the stability of modern manufacturing and service organizations, and in particular argues for a sense of urgency and continued reflection on quality standards. He identifies five areas of management which he argues constitute the essence of pro-active performance:

- an obsession with responsiveness to customers;
- constant innovation in all areas of the firm;
- partnership – the wholesale participation of and gainsharing with all people connected with the organization;
- leadership that loves change (instead of fighting it) and instils and shares an inspiring vision;
- control by means of simple support systems aimed at measuring the 'right stuff' for today's environment.

These areas are in line with earlier discussions in this chapter on implementing total quality, except perhaps that the initiation of change is given more emphasis. Yet markets change rapidly and competitors learn quickly, and a great deal of what affects industry is not always within the control of senior managers, and therefore has to be adapted to. This in itself entails managing significant changes through example and creates a need to encourage others to respond to and love change.

The ability to thrive on chaos and love change is, however, more in line with implementing TQM than might at first be anticipated. Anderson (1989) argues that quality management as a process must be continuous and never ending. He believes that accepting the concept of quality is a positive business strategy that offers a competitive edge in the market place. To succeed, however, there must be a commitment to quality improvement which goes well beyond putting in place quality assurance processes. Anderson suggests that in determining customers' needs there is no stability, and indeed customer satisfaction is strongly influenced by many non-product-related service issues. He counsels against documenting detailed specifications without recognizing and building in the ability to respond to change as reflected by customer expectations. Not only is this a powerful argument against over-emphasizing the importance of ISO 9000, but is also fully in line with Peters' thesis in terms of responding positively to change.

In conclusion, what emerges from the quality debate is that TQM is about people and not procedures. The emphasis placed on involving individuals in the ownership of their day-to-day activities is critical and is a means of delegating power while retaining managerial accountability. Developing quality systems depends on a management approach which releases individual creativity and innovation rather than on the introduction of procedures which impose conformity to standards. This recognizes that the emphasis on what customers require can in fact only be determined by asking them and engaging in some form of dialogue with them. To provide a framework within which customers are recognized by management and employees as being central, it is necessary to ensure that formal documented procedures are supplemented with individual creativity, freedom and responsibility. As ever, perhaps this is best summed up by Peters (1988) who suggests that: 'Every managerial act must be seen as an unequivocal support for urgency in pursuit of constant testing, change and improvement' (p 470).

References

Anderson, D N (1989) Quality, a positive business strategy. In J S Oakland (Ed) *Total Quality Management*. Bedford: IFS

Crosby, P B (1978) *Quality is Free. The Art of Making Quality Certain*. London: McGraw Hill

Crosby, P B (1989) *Let's Talk Quality*. London: McGraw Hill

Deming, W (1988) *Out of Crisis: Quality, Productivity and Competitive Position*. Cambridge: Cambridge University Press

Harvey, G (1989) The strategic implementation of total quality management. In J S Oakland (Ed) *Total Quality Management*. Bedford: IFS

Milner, S W (1990) Quality – What is it and why does it matter. *Teaching and Learning Bulletin* 3, 13–15

Oakland, D N (1989a) *Total Quality Management*. Bedford: (Ed) IFS

Oakland, D N (1989b) *Total Quality Management*. Oxford: Heinemann

Peters, T (1988) *Thriving on Chaos*. London: Macmillan

Peters, T and Waterman, R N (1982) *In Search of Excellence: Lesson from America's Best-Run Companies*. London: Harper and Row

Price, F (1984) *Right First Time: Using Quality Control for Profit*. Aldershot: Gower

2 Quality in Vocational Education and Training

The use of the term quality in education has been a noticeable feature of the late 1980s and has continued into the 1990s. It is interesting that many educational journals and publications refer specifically to the development of quality as one of the aims of education and, indeed, market it in its own right to both clients and providers (FEU, 1987; Miller and Dower, 1989). Within the public sector and especially in education, more and more job advertisements highlight qualitative output and stress the need to 'deliver' quality. It is also the case that although the term 'quality' is widely used, and some may argue it is easy to recognize, there is some evidence to suggest that it is extremely difficult to analyse conceptually and for there to be a shared understanding of the term (Müller and Funnell, 1991). Few of us involved with vocational education and training would deny that our aim is to deliver quality, although there is a considerable debate to be had concerning what quality is and how best to achieve it. The aim of this chapter is to explore quality in relationship to defining the product of education and its development.

Defining quality in education

In education, the term 'quality' has been used synonymously with effectiveness. It has also been interpreted as including efficiency and economy at the same time. Birch (1988), in what has become a significant source book for managers in vocational education, notes that effectiveness is concerned with outcomes and that 'a college is effective to the extent that it produces outcomes which are relevant to the needs and demands of its clients' (p 4). Although from a resourcing perspective the notion of effectiveness in this context seems reasonable, there is a major issue concerning the extent to which effectiveness, and hence quality, is being defined in resource terms, rather than from the perspective of achieving the desirable standard of output. It can be argued that outcomes which are relevant to the needs and demands of clients should be agreed in advance and met to the extent to which there are resources available. Hence, the effective provider is striving towards the optimum level of quality required but within a constrained resource base. This has not been teased out in publications such as that produced by Birch or commissioned by central government on managing colleges (DES, 1987). However, in this sense, quality can be seen as a legitimate aspiration of the educational system, whereas effectiveness can be measured in terms of the extent to which this has been achieved within financial constraints. It may therefore be seen as a more sophisticated way of bringing together the notions of effectiveness and efficiency into a coherent and comprehensive evaluative concept.

The Further Education Staff College (FESC) (1989) has produced a guide to work-based learning terms and in examining quality it is proposed that a variety of concepts are encompassed. These are identified as:

- meeting the personal development needs of the individual learner;
- meeting the skill requirements of employers according to established standards;
- consensus ideas as to what constitutes 'good' provision;
- within corporate planning, the cost of training, its effectiveness and short- and long-term added value (p 33).

These concepts lead to an emphasis on the 'inputs' and 'outcomes' of education and training. Measures of quality can be derived from the inputs into education which embrace the resource base, which include cost and the curriculum components necessary to design and deliver a programme of educational training. In terms of outcomes, emphasis can be given to the knowledge, skills, attitudes and general competences attained by the learner and the extent to which these meet the personal needs of the individual student and the requirements of employers. This emphasis on the verification of quality leads to the setting of clear and appropriate standards to meet client requirements and to building in processes of quality control to measure the extent to which the set standard has been attained. Thus, to a significant extent, the quality of training does depend on making explicit the criteria by which quality itself may be judged – a view which is put forward in the FESC guide (1989).

In contrast the Further Education Unit (FEU) has put forward a very strongly curriculum-related definition of quality which emphasizes the 'input' approach noted above (1987). It is argued that the quality of curricular provision depends on 'providing the right type of learning opportunities for those for whom we are obliged to provide' (p 4). Further emphasis is given to the need to provide accessible programmes of learning delivered in a supportive and facilitative environment, which at the same time lead to practical and relevant outcomes. Here the need to define in some way appropriate outcomes or standards is recognized, as well as the requirement to ensure that the curricular design process is taking account of measures of quality. Thus, the guiding principle for the work of the FEU is that the curriculum is central to the quality of education and is critical in putting into effect the concept of quality.

A more recent view has been offered by Her Majesty's Inspectorate in a Report to the Scottish Education Department on performance indicators for further education (HMI, 1990b). The Inspectorate established a definition of quality which included the following features : relevance, access, responsiveness, appropriateness of learning and teaching approaches and standards. These five features include a mixture of input and output variables. The emphasis on standards and relevance focuses on output, whereas it can be argued that the other features relate more specifically to input. Accessibility has also been highlighted by the FEU and, with its emphasis on relevance this contributes towards a curriculum-led perspective. This is indicative of the extent to which the concept of quality within further and vocational education is in itself highly sophisticated.

Another report by HM Inspectorate, on Science Education in the Polytechnics and Colleges (HMI,1990a), comments specifically on quality. It is noted that the quality of higher education science provision depends primarily on:

- the quality of the teaching and the learning it sustains;
- the efforts of teachers to keep themselves up to date through research and other scholarly activity through their contacts with, and knowledge of, developments in the science-based employment sectors;
- the quality of the resources available to support the teaching and learning;
- the rigour of the quality assurance and control procedures (p 18).

This is primarily an input approach to evaluating quality. The report also notes the importance of there being sufficient student numbers to justify a wide range of equipment, a broad range of staff and sufficiently large teaching groups to allow adequate peer interaction. The general conclusion reached is that in a great majority of cases the standards achieved by students are satisfactory. There is then a proposed link between input and output variables.

Day and Edwards (1990) have identified three 'confirmations' in seeking an understanding of the concept of quality, applied specifically, in their case, to higher education. First, there is a need to confirm the definition of quality which, while recognizing the importance of inputs, focuses more on the setting of appropriate standards and evaluating the extent to which they have been attained. Second, they point to the need to seek confirmation from customers in terms of making judgements of quality. In particular, three client groups are identified: students themselves; employers who in many cases second students on a part-time basis to gain further education and training; and the providers of funds, whether central government, local government or employers. The third confirmation they seek is the careful analysis of the products of the educational system, bearing in mind that large-scale educational providers are often multi-product organizations. As Day and Edwards rightly point out, unlike industry itself, 'customers' of further and vocational education are also the most important raw materials.

This analysis, employing an industrial model, points to the need to consider quality in terms of both input and output. The process of education needs systematizing in terms of product development, product delivery and, finally, quality control. The following section outlines a simple approach to viewing education in terms of creating products, to be consumed not only by individuals themselves, but for use by employers in providing services and generating wealth to support the economy.

Education and training: a product approach

Figures 2.1 and 2.2 illustrate a 'product' approach to vocational education and training. Figure 2.1, from Cave et al (1988), is derived from higher education whereas Figure 2.2, from Jones (1985), is more specific to vocational education and training. The models themselves demonstrate considerable differences in emphasis between further and higher education. The 'processing plant' model is set in a broader context and refers both to the wider resourcing issues and the internal structures required to facilitate the delivery of education and training. The model from Cave et al is simpler and enables inputs to be related to outputs in a very clear way. Nevertheless, it is important to try and tease out some of these differences in order to present a clearer picture of vocational education in terms of a product development approach.

In terms of inputs, it is important to recognize the raw material with which education has to work, that is, the students themselves. It is necessary to ensure that students are accessed on to courses which meet their short-term educational needs and longer-term career ambitions. Students bring with them a wealth of experience which often includes formal qualifications or relevant work experience. Once accessed into vocational education students are required to contribute endeavour, and therefore time, to the educational process. This is matched in many ways by the staff base both in terms of the quality of teaching as noted by the

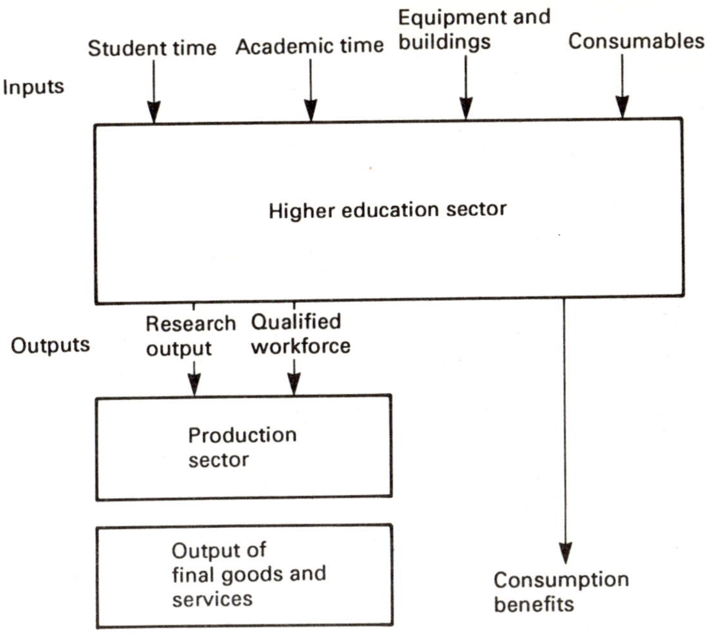

Figure 2.1 *Inputs and outputs in higher education* (Cave et al, 1988)

HMI Report on Higher Education and Science and the important role played by support staff especially those with specific student responsibilities such as technicians. In Jones' model this is incorporated into the internal structure of the processing plant whereas Cave et al refer specifically to academic time without making any specific reference to ancillary support staff in their diagrammatic representation of inputs into higher education. The importance of equipment, buildings and consumables is reflected in both models.

The outputs defined both for further and higher education might appear to be somewhat limited. For further education and vocational training the output is seen only in terms of qualified students without there being any recognition that those who part-qualify or gain from the educational process itself, can also contribute to the community through the production of goods or provision of services. The notion of added value is becoming of major importance in the UK in the light of the demographic trends and the significant resources invested in education and training in many European countries (Funnell and Müller, 1991). The 'intrinsic' benefits of education are included by Cave et al and are identified under 'consumption benefits'. It is predictable and proper that

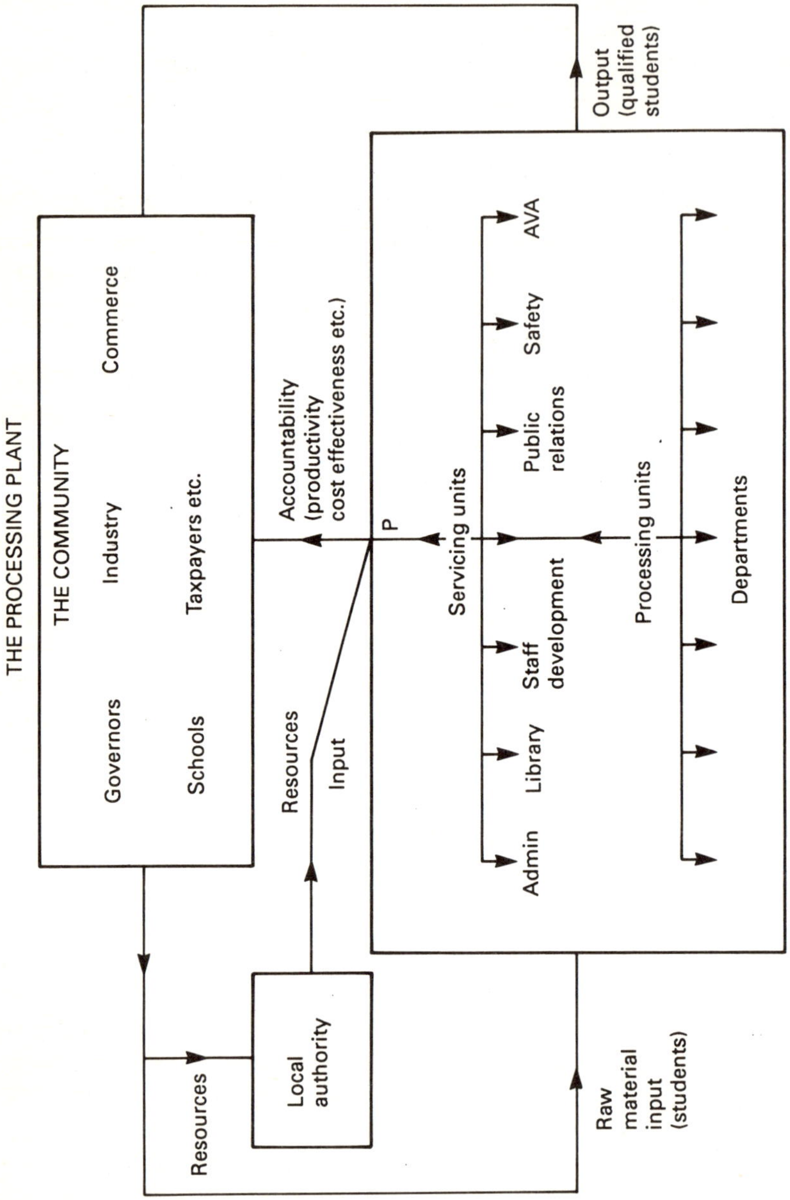

Figure 2.2 *The processing plant* (Jones, 1985)

for higher education there is a specific reference to research which is linked to the production sector. The concept of research here must be taken to include consultancy, which is offered to industry, commerce and the professions. However, it should be remembered that many universities are judged by the quality and quantity of their research publications, rather than by the value and impact research and consultancy has on society in general and the industrial sector specifically. The lack of reference to research or consultancy within the further education model is no longer accurate and there is now a major input into industry by Colleges of Further Education in a wide range of areas. In fact under the Education Reform Act it is now mostly a requirement that public sector institutions earn additional income in order to supplement the resources provided by central and local government.

This analysis suggests, however, that it is useful to look at vocational education and training in terms of product development. The resource base to support vocational education and training is changing and there is now a greater emphasis on supplementing public money with that provided by employers themselves (see Chapter 6). Within any individual organization these resources must be used efficiently and effectively to provide support and to facilitate student achievement. At the same time as working with students there are by-products of the educational process, including consultancy and research, which further contribute to the economic and social well-being of society. In the end, however, the overall process will be evaluated in terms of the extent to which it satisfies the perceived needs of individual students and the actual employment needs of industry, commerce and the professions.

Quality in product design

In line with the approach of the FEU it is necessary to place considerable emphasis on designing quality into the course-development process. The traditional curriculum-development model outlines a sequence to facilitate this process (see Hooper, 1971). This approach recognizes the importance of predetermining the broad aim of the course and stating the outcomes in terms of precise behavioural objectives. This leads on to the development of a curriculum that relates content and learning processes, and assessment procedures are then designed to test specifically the predetermined objectives. The final process, following successful recruitment to the course, is to put in place a systematic evaluation to judge the effectiveness of the total curriculum. In essence, this model is still valuable in putting together programmes of learning, but in terms of ensuring that quality is built into vocational education it is necessary to take into account more recent approaches to curriculum development.

Particular emphasis is now placed on how students are likely to participate in, and contribute to, the dynamic nature of any curriculum. This has been linked firmly to the vocational market and consideration has been given to the specific needs of employers and the broader needs of the economy. This is reflected in two pamphlets produced by the FEU (1987; 1989). The earlier pamphlet is derived from traditional approaches to curriculum design and describes a framework to facilitate the planning, design, delivery and evaluation of quality provision. The basis for this is the FEU model reflecting the processes of curriculum development (Figure 2.3). Underlying the design of a quality product is the identification of labour market needs, to ensure that the product reflects consultation with employers direct and other organizations such as Chambers of Commerce and, of course, Training and Enterprise Councils.

The more recent pamphlet *Towards a Framework for Curriculum*

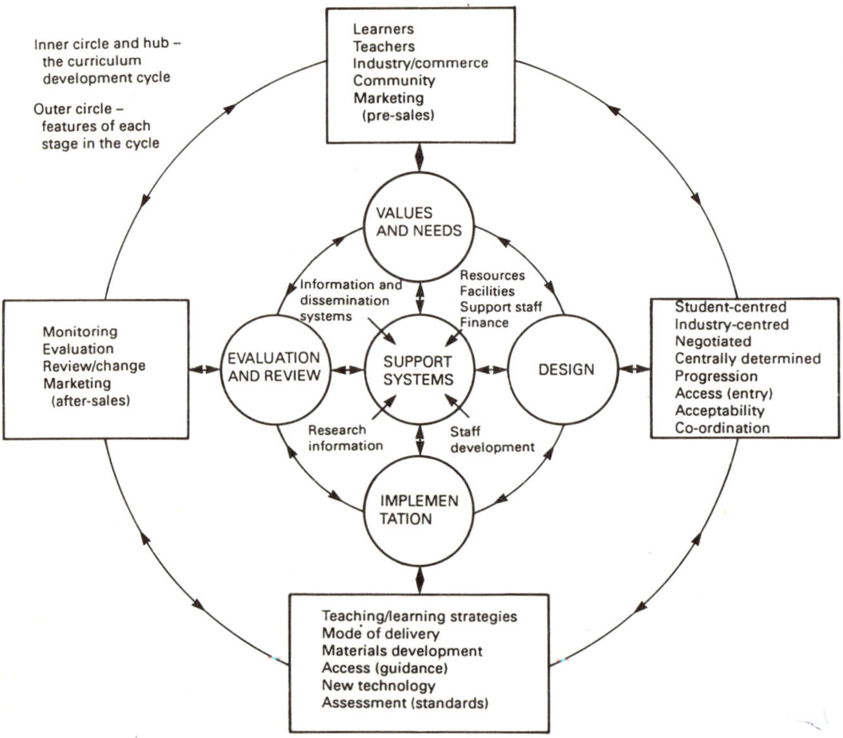

Figure 2.3 *FEU model of processes of curriculum development* (FEU, 1987)

Entitlement focuses more directly on the needs of learners with the view to enhancing the nature of teaching provided. This, it is argued, should be based on a common curriculum framework which aims to provide:

- appropriate learning opportunities, regardless of gender, race, age and ability;
- opportunities for all learners to establish and develop a recognised competence base of knowledge, skills and experience, sufficient to facilitate progression into employment, further education, training or other roles;
- an understanding of the local and national economic and social environment to promote an appreciation of the variety of available adult roles in society;
- a basis for learners to increase their self-awareness to appraise realistically their potential and prospects, and to become progressively responsible for negotiating their own personal development (p 7).

These themes are summarized in terms of three generic learning themes: relevance; flexibility; and the development of competence. This approach recognizes much more the role individuals play in negotiating their own learning strategies (see Chapter 5). It puts forward a model whereby individuals take greater responsibility for their programme of study, within which there is a clear curriculum entitlement. The needs of employers are reflected through predetermining the curriculum entitlement in such a way as to link the ambitions and abilities of individual students to the needs of the work place.

The notion of a curriculum entitlement related to employers' needs is the basis of the report made by the National Curriculum Council to the Secretary of State on the introduction of core skills for those aged 16–19 (NCC, 1990). This response shifts the balance away from the individual student towards the perceived and identified needs of employers. The NCC recognizes the need to develop all young people in such a way as to equip them for the world of work and to foster the development of vocational work-based skills. Six skills are identified:

- communication;
- problem solving;
- personal skills;
- numeracy;
- information technology;
- modern language competence.

This is a different way to determine a curriculum entitlement and one which it could be argued meets the clear needs of employers. It is not, however, without problems, both of a conceptual and practical nature (see

Chapter 4). On the other hand few educationists would argue with the core skills which have been identified and those of us committed to developing European initiatives particularly welcome the introduction of a modern language. The NCC also recommends that special emphasis be placed on ensuring continuity across the whole of the educational system and in maximizing progression to as high a level of achievement as is possible. As well as proposing the identification of attainment targets, providers are encouraged to develop modular credit accumulation and transfer schemes to link together and bridge the unnecessary divide between academic and vocational education (see Chapter 12).

It is possible to bring together these diverse yet related approaches to the development of quality in vocational education by identifying critical issues which course designers need to confront. One of these design features is that of increasing *participation* both in further and higher education. Smithers and Robinson (1989) recognize the importance of establishing links between further and higher education and in particular focus on Access Courses to encourage more students to progress into higher education. The '*access movement*' has now become more established and institutionalized (Loew, 1989). Many students receive formal grants and there is now a commitment nationally to provide Access courses targeted specifically at mature students. Linked to this is the 'Accreditation of Prior Learning' which is a means of accrediting prior experience towards a further or higher educational qualification. It is recognized that many people acquire considerable skills through workplace and other life-experience and that traditionally the educational system has not allowed this to count towards a formal qualification. The 'Accreditation of Prior Learning' seeks to redress this and, taken together, these design features incorporate a wider commitment to equal opportunities.

Once students have been accessed on to courses there has emerged a clear commitment to structure the learning environment to meet the needs of the individual student. Considerable emphasis is now placed on developing *autonomy* and in encouraging students to negotiate their own learning. Learning is judged to be more effective when active and when it engages the student as a partner in the learning process. Quality, in designing a course, is also judged by the extent to which there is continuity between previous learning and experience and the new programme of study. *Continuity* and *progression* taken together help students to maximize their potential and move up the educational ladder by taking appropriate-sized steps. Unlike many European countries, the UK does not enable all qualified students to progress into higher education, or even into further and vocational education. There is no right of continuity or progression. Yet, the establishment of these features into the design of courses would maximize the opportunities currently available to the student market.

Delivering quality educational products

As already discussed, the essence of the quality approach to management is in providing products which meet the exact specifications of the customer. Quality is about providing what the customer wants. In the context of vocational education and training this raises two fundamental issues: first, what is the product of vocational education? and second, who is the customer?

It should also be noted at this stage that the product of education is not independent of the consumer in that he or she participates actively in creating and redefining the product. There is an inherent link between the direct customer of vocational education and what it is trying to provide.

It can be argued that the products of vocational education and training are becoming more clearly defined (FESC, 1989). It is clear that consumers and employers expect vocational education and training to provide knowledge and basic skills. These outcomes have more recently been redefined in terms of competencies. In simple terms competencies are work-based skills required by specific occupational groups. The use of competencies as defining the outcomes of vocational education is not without difficulty or controversy (Burke, 1990). Nevertheless, the emphasis on occupational and employer-led skills which are assessed in the work place has been fundamental in the gradual movement during the last five years to an employer-led model of vocational education and training. The implications for vocational education and training providers and for the delivery of quality products is considered in Chapter 11.

It has also been recognized that vocational education and training do need to provide more generic skills of an interpersonal nature. The recent report of the NCC discussed earlier reflects this. It is more difficult to define the product of education in terms of attitudes or interpersonal abilities. All employers and, one suspects, students themselves, desire education and training to provide high-level interpersonal skills in order to develop personal effectiveness and entrepreneurial behaviour. It can be suggested that these skills can be built into the course design through facilitating participative approaches to learning and teaching. This approach is explicit in the educational philosophy of the 'Capability Movement' which is to encourage learners to exercise responsibility, take initiatives and to become creative individuals (Stephenson, 1988). The 'Education for Capability Movement' which has been sponsored by the Royal Society of Arts, focuses on the development of problem-solving skills and different modes of inquiry, including scientific and aesthetic (Burgess, 1985).

Perhaps the critical feature of developing high-level interpersonal skills and capable, trained individuals is the development of flexibility. It is now increasingly recognized that a large majority of the work force will have to acquire significant new skills at least once after having commenced work. It is also increasingly recognized that it is entirely reasonable to expect individuals to contribute more widely in employment. This requires maximum flexibility within and between individuals, and a commitment to developing generic occupational skills rather than those which meet the needs of only one specific occupational group. There is a place for the latter, but it must be developed in line with ensuring that we develop a capable and flexible work force.

The second question is at one level simple, but at another complex. It is relatively easy to identify three groups of customers concerned with the products of vocational education and training. At a superordinate level the ultimate customer might be seen as the provider of funds, which is either central or local government, supplemented by employer and student contributions. More specifically, employers can be seen as customers in that they support a large proportion of students studying part-time in vocational education. And yet the immediate recipient of education and training, and the customer who paradoxically contributes to the process itself, is the student.

One useful way of looking at this is in terms of the sophistication used by each customer group to evaluate the quality of education and training. The most distant, and yet strategically and politically the most significant, is central government. Central government is responsible for agreeing set standards, as in the case of the National Curriculum and for the structure of the educational system itself. The products of education are seen as raw material in terms of the needs of industry. Education serves a specific purpose which can be seen as developing individuals in such a way that they can contribute creatively to the future needs of the country. In evaluating quality, special emphasis has been placed on collecting large-scale data, which is qualified by the more direct approach carried out by HM Inspectorate (HMI). The role of HMI is perhaps less clear now than it was ten years ago. Nevertheless, by sampling specific public sector educational provision, HMI serves to provide qualitative data to support the quantitative information generated by large surveys. It remains an anomaly that the university sector is not subject to HMI.

The Education Reform Act has led to Local Authorities defining quite precisely the factors which will be used to make judgements about the further and higher education for which they have a strategic responsibility. These are primarily based on a notion of efficiency, as discussed above, rather than quality. Hence, the main measures tend to be quantitative including, for example, completion rates for students enrolled on courses, the average cost of each full-time equivalent student completing the course, qualifications gained, and employment rates or progression to further and higher education. Although there has been a significant increase in Inspectors employed by Local Authorities, the Education Reform Act places only a strategic responsibility on Local Authorities to oversee quality and it is within their powers to delegate this entirely to educational providers.

Employers are more likely to measure the quality of education in line with the extent to which their occupational needs are met. Many employers financially sponsor students to study part-time or even full-time and therefore have a vested interest in the immediate product of education. It is absolutely clear that in order to be competitive within Europe and elsewhere, particularly following the completion of the Single European Market, there will be a need to increase the provision of education and training significantly. There is an inherent conflict in this position. The demographic trends are such that there are fewer young people available in the workplace and employers are tempted to offer considerable financial rewards to encourage young people to take up employment. At the same time, unless these young people acquire marketable skills, there is the danger that industry will become uncompetitive, unemployment will rise and the economy stagnate. There has to be a means of ensuring that employers recognize their responsibilities for facilitating education and training. The short-term needs of employers are not the long-term needs of the economy.

The customer group most intimately involved with the educational process, and more specifically with the quality of delivery and outcome, is the student group. Students are in a position to feed information of a more sophisticated and detailed kind into the evaluation process. In Chapter 3, Barnett argues that central to the whole process of quality control is putting the student first. It is of course difficult for students themselves, while they are inherently part of the educational process, to evaluate themselves as products of the educational system. Such reflection is only possible at a much later stage, presumably once they are employed or participating as active members of the community. Nevertheless, students can have a direct impact on the quality of educational provision and therefore have both a right and a responsibility to contribute constructively to this debate.

It therefore becomes imperative to take an institutional perspective on evaluating the quality of provision. The use of BS 5750, which as noted in Chapter 1, sets out a comprehensive series of requirements which suppliers must meet in order to be registered, is a narrow and rather restrictive approach to the evaluation of quality. The use of performance indicators (DES, 1987; Cave et al, 1988) is a means of providing quantitative data on the basis of which judgements relating to quality can be derived. Yet in themselves performance indicators tend to be one step removed from evaluating the teaching and learning process (Elton, 1987). They do not appear to put at the heart of the evaluation process the educational and training needs of the student and the impact trained personnel have when commencing employment. In Chapter 6, Bax explores the value of systematically evaluating the impact recently trained personnel have in the workplace as a means of supporting educational providers in designing relevant, yet challenging curricula. For there to be an effective system for evaluating quality, it must be given priority at senior management level within educational and training institutions. The process should be one of encouraging full participation from educational providers, employers and students in such a way that the responsibility for ensuring quality is devolved to each and every participating individual linked to the organization. This in fact is the essence of the 'Total Quality Management' approach explored in Chapter 1, which focuses specifically on identifying and meeting the requirements of the customer.

Conclusion

The major themes of this Chapter are developed in the rest of this book, focusing on students as customers, employers as customers, and institutional approaches to implementing quality assurance. Underpinning this analysis is a view that without including customers as part of the quality assurance process it will not be possible within an educational and training context to deliver products which meet the predicted employer needs of the 1990s and beyond.

References

Birch, D (1988) *Managing Resources in Further Education: A Handbook for College Managers*. Bristol: FESC
Burgess, T (Ed) (1985) *Education for Capability*. Windsor: NFER
Burke, J (Ed) (1990) *Competency Based Education and Training*. London: Falmer
Cave, M; Hanney, S; Kogan, M; and Trevett, G (1988) *The Use of Performance Indicators in Higher Education*. London: Jessica Kingsley
Day, B and Edwards, T (1990) Quality in Higher Education – the industrial approach. *Teaching and Learning Bulletin* 3, 6–10
DES (1987) *Managing Colleges Efficiently*. London: HMSO
Elton, L (1987) Warning signs. *THES* 11 September, 12
FESC (1989) *A Guide to Work Based Learning Terms*. London: HMSO
FEU (1987) *Quality in NAFE*. London: DES
FEU (1989) *Towards a Framework for Curriculum Entitlement*. London: DES

Funnell, P and Müller D J (1991) *Vocational Education and the Challenge of Europe.* London: Kogan Page

HMI (1990a) *Higher Education in the Polytechnics and Colleges. Science.* London: HMSO

HMI (1990b) *Management of Educational Resources: 3. Measuring Up: Performance Indicators in Further Education.* London: HMSO

Hooper, R (Ed) (1971) *The Curriculum: Context, Design and Development.* Edinburgh: Oliver and Boyd

Jones, D (1985) Efficient effectiveness in Colleges – A practical approach. *Coombe Lodge Report* 18, 138–50

Loew, S (Ed) (1989) *Access to Higher Education.* London: South Bank Polytechnic

Miller, J and Dower, A (1989) *Improving Quality in Further Education.* London: Dept. of Employment

Müller, D J and Funnell P (1991) Quality in vocational education. In R Winterburn (Ed) *Aspects of Educational and Training Technology, XXIV.* London: Kogan Page

NCC (1990). *Core Skills 16–19.* York: NCC

Smithers, A and Robinson, P (1989) *Increasing Participation in Higher Education.* London: British Petroleum

Stephenson, J (1988) Higher Education for capability. The challenge. *Paper presented at RSA on 22 November to launch 'Education for Capability'*

PART II

Quality: Students as Clients

The three Chapters in Part II explore the theme of quality from the student perspective. Whether or not one considers that it is employers, those who provide central or local funding, or students who are the main customers of education, it is absolutely clear that the major participant in the process of education and training is the student learner. We have already explored the intricacies of a process of teaching and learning in which the customer is also the product. The significance of this in terms of curriculum design cannot, and should not, be under-emphasized. Students by their own behaviour play a major role in creating the outcomes or products of the educational process and therefore are symbiotic in the teaching and learning relationship.

A response to the recognition of the role which students play in their creation of the educational product, has been to highlight the process of teaching and learning. Hence there is considerable research evaluating different modes of teaching styles and the ways in which students themselves as individuals react (Richardson et al, 1987). Equally important, in terms of evaluating the quality of education, is placing the student at the centre of this process and in doing so to transfer some of the responsibility for the product to the customer. This then places the emphasis on what the customer needs and wants to learn rather than on what the teachers or tutors wish to teach.

Barnett, in his closely argued contribution (Chapter 3), takes as central the role of the student in higher education. He argues that those with the responsibility for managing an institution must do so on the basis of its prime client group, that is, the students themselves. This places a responsibility on educational managers and tutors to develop and implement processes which retain the centrality of the student experience.

In this approach, what becomes of major importance, is the teacher/student relationship, the ways in which the institution enhances the ability and skills of its staff and the ways in which students are encouraged to participate fully in the learning process. Using this model Barnett argues against seeing higher education in terms of vocational training but recognizes the importance of making it easy for students to go beyond the simple learning of skills to being able to reflect upon these critically. This he refers to as 'vocational education'.

The vocational aspects of delivering quality education to students is the theme explored by Muir (Chapter 4). He reviews contemporary perspectives on introducing a core curriculum for all those above the age of 16 who will be continuing their studies. This core curriculum is derived from the perceptions of employers that young people should possess a range of generic, transferable skills. From the students' perspective, implicit in this initiative, is the development of personal abilities which are not subject-specific, but which enable them to negotiate their own processes of learning and final outcomes within broad external guidelines. In recognizing the importance of generic, interpersonal skills and in building them into the curriculum, the role of subject-specific knowledge is likely to be given less emphasis. Therefore, students will be encouraged to delay their specialized choices until a later date and will retain 'ownership' of their educational development until such time as they select a particular vocational occupation. The implications for the ways in which students engage with the core curriculum are as yet under-explored, but are likely to have a major impact on vocational education and training into the 1990s.

The development of a core curriculum in conjunction with putting the student as customer at the centre of the educational process leads into further consideration of an 'entitlement' curriculum. The Further Education Unit (FEU, 1989) has outlined the arguments for the development of a 'learners' curriculum entitlement'. It is argued that: 'learners should be allowed to negotiate their own interim targets for achievement within nationally agreed parameters and mechanisms by which this will be checked' (p 11). This approach places considerable emphasis on outcomes which are seen to be in the ownership of the student as 'customer'. Each individual learner is entitled to negotiate a learning contract which the FEU document perceives as being in terms of a learning plan describing content, outcomes, progression and experiences. Such a framework encourages the student to negotiate a programme within agreed external parameters and hence to take ownership of the curriculum and therefore the learning process.

This approach is taken a step further by Hinds in Chapter 5. She describes the Independent Study programme at the Polytechnic of East

London which allows and encourages students to design their own curriculum, including content, methods of learning and assessment procedures. This approach recognizes in a radical way that the individual student is personally responsible for the product and is therefore entitled to create the outcomes of the educational process which he or she judges to be appropriate and to match his or her needs. The School for Independent Study at the Polytechnic of East London does not provide courses, but rather a framework which enables students to design their own programme of study from start to finish. Furthermore, tutors are seen as facilitators of this process and therefore causal in developing the process of learning. Considerable emphasis is placed upon the drawing up of a 'learning contract' along the lines recognized by the Further Education Unit. With the introduction of Training Credits and of innovative programmes combining traditional A levels with vocational courses, the use of individually negotiated learning contracts is likely to increase over the next decade. The pioneering work described by Hinds and currently being extended to the Suffolk College, is an excellent model of how best to put the student at the centre of the educational process, not only as part of the system, but as its major product.

In putting the student at the centre of the educational production system it is interesting to note that neither the core curriculum nor the outcomes of the educational process are prescribed in terms of subject specialisms but in terms of student qualities. The language of education and training is changing in such a way that the student is being given ownership of the process of learning. Students are striving to develop entrepreneurial and problem-solving skills which enable them to deal readily with a wide range of situations. They are being encouraged to take responsibility for their own learning and to become involved in all the components which traditionally make up the curriculum. Education and training is not being developed along the lines of something which happens to the individual made possible by tutors, but rather as a framework created by students themselves within which they have ownership of the outcomes. This autonomy and freedom to negotiate must be seen as a critical product of the 'new' approaches to education and training and yet is in line with the demands of employers for the development of generic and interpersonal skills and competencies. The paradox is that in determining externally the vocational requirements of employers, both the government and employer associations are enabling students to take more responsibility and to become more autonomous in the process of becoming a 'marketable' commodity.

This 'movement' parallels the development of 'Total Quality Management' in which responsibility for and ownership of the quality of the product is devolved as far as is feasible to the workforce itself. By making the student the focus of the educational process, it can be argued that quality is being built into vocational education and training. Hence, 'total quality' is in the ownership of the student and in principle leads to a 'zero defect' output. Learning outcomes have been negotiated and determined in advance rather than being inspected out by a series of non-negotiable traditional assessment procedures. Radical as this may seem, it is entirely in line with the 'quality movement'. It suggests opportunities for major advances in the delivery of quality vocational education and training but only if educationalists and trainers are prepared and able to give up their ownership of students' learning. Chapters 3 to 5 suggest strongly that unless we put the student at the heart of the educational process we cannot expect to deliver high quality vocational education and training.

References

FEU (1989) *Towards a Framework for Curriculum Entitlement*. London: Further Education Unit

Richardson, J T E, Eysenck, M W and Piper, D W (1987) *Student Learning. Research in Education and Cognitive Psychology*. Society for Research into Higher Education and Open University: Milton Keynes

3 Delivering Quality in Student Learning

Ronald Barnett

Three questions are paramount in the matter of delivering quality in student learning:

- What is 'quality' in relation to student learning?
- How can we promote it?
- How do we know that we have been successful in producing high quality student learning?

I shall take each of these issues in turn, but one other point has to be brought out first. Answering these questions cannot be just a technical matter. These are not questions simply of logic or of empirical investigation. For, ultimately, what we mean by 'quality' in regard to student learning is bound up with our values and fundamental aims in vocational education (Badley, 1989a). We cannot begin to be precise about quality in this domain without taking up a value position, connected with what we take vocational education to be. In turn, what we take vocational education to be will have implications for how we conceive of student learning, how we promote it, and how we evaluate our success in achieving it.

In this situation, there are two options in front of us. An attempt could be made to tease out, in a neutral fashion, different conceptions of student learning as they derive from varying conceptions of vocational education, and to follow through their logic for the curriculum and subsequent evaluation. Or, perhaps more risky, an attempt could be made to take up and argue for a particular position. It is that latter course that I will follow here.

What is 'quality' in student learning?

The very idea of quality

There is a sense in which the sheer application of the term 'quality' in relation to student learning is somewhat otiose. For learning is something one can do under one's own steam, at home, on the train, in the local library, or even at the sports centre. It can be done under one's own direction, in other words. More than that, it can be undertaken for its own sake, without any other end in view. It can even happen unexpectedly, when one learns something of substance, say, in a documentary on the television.

Now, it is possible to apply the idea of 'quality' to learning in these circumstances; but it would be somewhat inappropriate. We may be able to say that this person actually learnt more from that book on that train journey than that person, or learnt with more understanding. But if the learning was never undertaken with a view to its being assessed; if it is something one just does, for the pleasure or satisfaction it brings, then the application of the idea of 'quality' is entirely out of place. The individual simply applies him- or herself to the task, and may have no interest in knowing about the quality of the learning that results.

This observation indicates that talk of 'quality' of student learning has point in circumstances *other* than those in which learning is entirely self-motivated and is purely under the control of the learner and using simply the learner's own resources. We apparently become interested in the quality of learning where public resources are at stake, and where there is a desire to ensure that those resources are being used to proper effect. It is where those offering the facilities for learning are subject to processes of *accountability* that a concern arises with the quality of the learning which is taking place.

It may be said that the conclusion does not follow from the premises. It is surely the case, some might say, that all teachers should feel a professional concern with the quality of their teaching. Whether public resources are being used or not, whether in formal educational settings or not, all teachers should want to establish how effective their teaching is, and should want to determine that their students have achieved a high quality of learning. That may be so as a principle, but two things need to be said in response.

First, the contemporary concern in education with the quality of learning is, as a matter of fact, directed to formal educational settings. At the level of higher education, for instance, the two new funding councils for the universities and polytechnics and colleges have signalled their interest in the quality of teaching as a criterion in judging bids for funds from institutions. Second, the objection helps to make part of the point I am making. A concern with the quality of learning comes into play when there is present someone (a teacher) or some set of resources (an educational institution) in addition to the learner. 'Quality of learning' comes on to the agenda as the other side of the coin of 'quality of teaching';

when, in other words, those responsible for the curriculum feel a need to demonstrate to some body other than the student that high quality learning has been achieved.

All of this may seem an unnecessarily abstract digression in getting to grips with improving quality of student learning in vocational education. There is, though, a significant point to be drawn from these observations, which is that the sheer application of the concept of quality may have underlying motivations which are imported from outside the teaching and learning situation. When we hear the term 'quality' being employed, we should stop and ask: who is using the term? What interests are behind its use?

Differing views of quality

I shall develop the point more fully later on; but the point just made deserves some justification now, however brief. Here, I pick up the claim I made at the outset, that putting the language of 'quality' into operation necessarily involves a conception of what we take vocational education to be, and that the underlying conception and its associated values will in turn lead to particular ways of assessing 'quality'. For example, if we conceive of vocational educational education as a process of fulfilling particular slots in the labour market with individuals who are going to be 'productive', then one way of assessing quality of learning might be to examine the destinations of the students. Not just whether they are employed; but are they employed in the kinds of position envisaged by the course designers? Further, can we derive measures of the productivity of those diplomats in the labour market? Here, for example, we might want to look at the economic rates of return of those graduates over, say, a ten-year period: allowing for the opportunity costs and the costs of their education, does it appear that their education has generated extra economic added-value?

That is one way of assessing the quality of the learning that has taken place. But if we start from a different value position, a different form of assessing the 'quality' of the learning may result. If we believe that quality of learning is more demonstrated in the depth of understanding that students achieve, in their ability to be self-critical, and in their capacity to apply that understanding and self-critical capacity to all they experience and do, then 'quality' of learning takes on a quite different character. Under this conception, 'quality' will be assured by a set of carefully designed assessments that do actually examine the students in these domains, as well as simply their grasp of factual knowledge or their ability to perform satisfactorily under particular determinable conditions.

These conceptual distinctions point us towards a further aspect in relation to the vocabulary of 'quality'. 'Quality control' is a term which is often employed in evaluation in the field of vocational education. But the idea of 'control' has to be absolutely repudiated. If what we have in mind when we talk of learning quality is what should be going on in the minds of the students at the end of their courses, and if we are seriously in the business of vocational 'education' as distinct from training, control can have no place at all. For a truly educational process is essentially unpredictable.

In a genuinely educational transaction, no one can precisely predict how individuals will react to the experiences put their way. And this is exactly as it should be. An educational process, particularly where young adults are involved, will look to enable those going through it to be able to stand on their own two feet, to be articulate about their thoughts and experiences, and to be able literally to give an account of their own (that is, what they themselves own). In short, they have to be their own selves. Concepts of integrity, authenticity and autonomy have to come into play. There has ultimately to be an open-mindedness in any really educational process. So the idea of 'control', even 'quality control', is inapposite. On the contrary, we want to produce an educational process which is uncontrolled, in the sense that the students' responses are their own.

Beyond teaching and learning

Something rather surprising follows from this observation. It is that the quality of teaching is not a good in itself. A necessary condition of effective teaching is that it has to lead on to effective student learning. This is not to say that an effective teacher has to provide some *a priori* guarantee that his or her efforts will produce effective learning in every student; the point just made about the student's inner consciousness being an interdependent variable vitiates any such guarantees. But there is a symbiotic relationship between effective teaching and effective learning; some of the latter has to be going on for the former to be present. And effective student learning has to include achieving the kinds of student autonomy that I have just sketched out (Baird, 1988).

The point can be driven further in relation to the concept of learning. Yes, we want our students in vocational education to learn that such and such is thc casc, and how to accomplish particular objectives. But vocational education – as distinct from vocational training – is accomplished when students are able to reflect on their learning, to evaluate it critically, and to take up stances towards it. It emerges, then, that while learning, too, is necessary, it is not sufficient. At least at the higher levels of vocational education, the student on graduating should be – in a sense – freed from his or her learning, so that what has been learnt can be put into service as a resource. Even if intended for use in a particular occupation, the learning should have been taken on board in such a way that it can be later deployed intelligently, and perhaps ultimately rejected as later life-long learning supersedes it.

So it turns out that not only teaching, but even learning itself has to be treated with caution, if we are interested in promoting the quality of learning in vocational education.

Different kinds of learning

To put the point in less abstract terms, it is increasingly recognized that we can no longer be satisfied in inculcating subject-specific knowledge and skills in our students. General transferable skills, many believe, must be imparted as well. Certainly, that claim leaves open many questions, such as: what precisely is meant by 'transferable skills'? do they, in fact, exist independently of their realization in specific domains of activity and thought? can they be taught by themselves, outside particular contexts, requiring specific knowledge and skills for their realization? are there differences, as some maintain, between general personal skills and general intellectual skills?

This is not the place to become enmeshed in the interstices of those complex issues. The point is surely made, in any case. If we want our students, on leaving their courses, to be able to make their way in a changing world, with unforeseen patterns of demand and expectation, with its shifting relationships between work and non-work activities, and with the complexities of global citizenship becoming more insistent, then narrow subject-specific knowledge and skills can no longer provide a sufficient means of framing a curriculum (if, indeed, they ever did). Students have to be given general frameworks of thought and action which enable them to transcend particular and bounded frameworks. As well as learning that, and learning how, they need to be able – where it is appropriate – to discard their learning as such, and learn how to leave it behind them.

It follows from this discussion that in improving the quality of student learning we cannot focus our efforts simply on improving the quality of teaching as if it were an entity in itself. But it also follows, paradoxically, that we cannot even concentrate on improving the quality of student learning, if by that we have in mind simply improving the student's acquisition of subject-specific knowledge and skills. General intellectual capacities *and* general personal skills also have to be improved.

We have then, on this analysis, four domains in which improvement of learning should take place:

- subject-specific knowledge;
- subject-specific skills;

- general intellectual capacities;
- general personal skills.

Unless our efforts to secure higher quality in student learning are addressed to each of those four domains, those efforts are likely to be deficient in some degree or other.

Any effort to bring about high quality learning in those areas has, though, first to be based on a prior conception of what is to count as 'high quality' learning in each domain. I offer some brief indications here.

Quality of understanding

In being clear about learning in the domain of subject-specific knowledge, it is worth drawing on a central strand of international research into student learning over the past 20 years (Marton, 1984). Conducted particularly in the UK, Sweden, and Australia, the research has shown that individual students tend to adopt different learning styles. At the extreme, two styles are contrasted: using a 'deep' approach, the student tries to form a personal insight into his or her learning experiences; in contrast, the student who employs a 'surface' approach is motivated much more to be able to memorize and to reproduce what he or she has experienced. To that finding – replicated across subjects, across different kinds of curricula, and across countries – we should add another and perhaps more significant finding. This is that those different learning styles are not just a matter of different personality structures among students, but are much more the outcome of the kind of curriculum experience with which students are faced.

Their learning style is a rational attempt to come to terms with the demands placed on them. One student taking a two-subject course may adopt a deep learning approach for one subject and a surface approach for the other. Against findings of this kind, giving students study skills courses to encourage a shift to a deep learning approach can only be a palliative (Entwistle, 1989). What is required is a fundamental rethink on the part of those who design the course, for two reasons. First, the aim should be directly to prompt higher order analytic and critical capacities which require a deep learning approach. Second, there should be a willingness to give students greater insight into their own learning strategies, and so produce 'metacognition' as it is termed (Baird, 1988). In this way, students can be more in command of their own learning styles and they will be enabled to maximize the effectiveness of their learning.

For our present purposes, the key lesson to be gleaned from that research is that it is not just the student's learning style that is affected by the curriculum experience; more profoundly, the student's level of comprehension and understanding is heavily influenced by the situation in which he or she is placed. So if we are concerned with the quality of learning in the domain of subject-specific knowledge, we have to try to design a curriculum which is likely to encourage students to adopt a deep-learning approach to the material they come across.

To do this, we have to find ways of reducing the pressures which promote 'reproducing' and 'surface' approaches, so lessening the student's concern merely to assimilate factual material in order to reproduce it in closed examinations. Two strategies need to be pursued at once. The anxiety which prompts students to adopt 'reproducing' learning strategies has to be lightened by ensuring that the sheer workload and assessment demands do not overburden students. And the students have to be actively involved in their own learning. Passive learning situations should be reduced, and students encouraged to learn – with suitable guidance – by themselves or in groups (Badley, 1989a; Baird, 1988; Entwistle, 1989).

I turn to the other domain involving intellectual capacities, that of general intellectual skills. Under such a heading we might put analytic skills; being able to integrate material and see relationships; being able to form critical evaluations; and being able to place one's learning in a wider context. All of these abilities amount to this: the educated person should be able to form a view of his or her learning experiences, and not be entirely caught up in it, but be able to stand back, and see it under different aspects. These are high-level abilities, and not always achieved.

A major study by Perry in the USA has shown that students do tend to move along a path of intellectual formation, which we might characterize as moving from a fixed perception of truth to a relativistic stance (Perry, 1970). It is accompanied by a shift from a sense of knowledge as external and as given, to an appreciation of the student's own involvement in his or her truth claims and, therefore, of their essentially negotiated character. Perry has identified a series of stages in this intellectual growth, but – as he points out – not all students reach the ultimate stages. Often they become fixed in their intellectual growth at some intermediate stage.

Against this analysis of intellectual growth, a key question for those involved in vocational education is: how far up this sequential path, within vocational education, should we expect our students to go? Are we simply to be content with our students having reached the stage, say, of recognizing that truth claims change over time and that they need to have the flexibility to take on new kinds of knowledge?

Are we to suppose that the kinds of occupation in which successful diplomats are likely to find themselves call for just that level of insight and no more? Or are we to raise our expectations higher and believe that all students who receive some kind of advanced education in preparation for their place in modern post-industrial society need to advance to the highest level of intellectual growth. All fully participating citizens, in other words, need to be able to challenge truth claims themselves, and in their own professional domains should feel that they have a hand in participating, and in continually reframing the responsibilities and the knowledge base of their profession.

Bound up, then, with our aims in vocational education are our attitudes to the framing and distribution of knowledge in society: is it largely a process conducted by a small élite or is it a democratic process in which all engaged in a profession are involved? But our aspirations for vocational education, and our conceptions of the capacities of our students, are also connected with our fundamental conception of human nature. Do we believe that all persons in society have a legitimate entitlement to exert their own powers of critical reason, and to share in society's continuing redefinition of its values and policies? Or do we think that those capacities are given to just a few (perhaps those who have experienced higher education in its highest and purest forms) while those who have experienced a strictly vocational education are more destined to accept the framework of societal conceptions with which they are presented? Certainly, there is nothing in Perry's work which suggests that the highest stages of intellectual growth are beyond those students who undergo a purely vocational education.

Quality in action

The preceding paragraphs have given some insight into what high quality might mean in relation to students' intellectual formation, whether subject-specific or of a more general character. The question remains, can we identify a parallel scheme for the development of the student's skills, again whether subject-specific or whether we have in mind general transferable skills? To some extent, this is the province in the UK of the National Council for Vocational Qualifications (NCVQ) and of the Training Agency (TA) in their sponsorship of a 'competency' approach to vocational education (Burke, 1989). I cannot, though, endorse the path taken for that programme, for its logic seems to run counter to that which I have traced for the student's intellectual formation. In the realm of intellectual capacities, we can talk, for example, of a student's continuing greater understanding, ever-widening insight, and expanding preparedness to be involved in his or her own truth claims. In other words, we can conceive of intellectual growth as just that: a continuing process of development, which can go on all through one's life. It remains an open question, I believe, whether or not we can identify a corresponding series of stages of growth in the field of skills which match that which holds for the growth of understanding. This seems to be implicitly recognized in the approach of the NCVQ and the TA, in their conceptualization of a competence-based curriculum. For there, the issue in each unit and for each objective is simply whether the competence in question has been realized. It is a yes/no situation: either the technique at stake has been mastered or it has not.

Admittedly, a gradation of achievement in relation to competence is evident in the hierarchy of levels which the NCVQ is mapping out in different occupational areas. But what differentiates the levels is less a complexity of skills *per se*, as the incorporation at the higher levels of increasing degrees of knowledge, understanding, and general personal qualities such as leadership. This conceptualization of higher level *skills* in terms of their integration of *knowledge* and understanding is evident in the assessment of practical training where it occurs in higher education. For there we are witnessing an approach to assessment which precisely attempts to identify the understanding which lies behind a particular activity on the part of the student. For example, in teacher education, students on teaching practice are being asked to follow their classroom performance with an articulated account of their experience. Either orally or through producing a logbook, they are expected to display the reasoning behind their actions, the various alternative courses of action that were considered and their critical evaluation of the way in which things turned out. Similar developments are taking place in the training element of business studies courses. Clearly, such self-reflection and self-critical capacities are susceptible to an ever greater sophistication, and cannot adequately be captured by a simple yes/no categorization. But it is the student's application of his/her knowledge, insight, and self-understanding that point to a more complex method of assessment, not the performance itself.

Promoting high quality student learning

The promotion of high quality student learning takes place at three distinct levels within an institution of further or higher education: that of the teacher in interacting with the students on a course; of the host department; and of the institution itself (Elton, 1990). In short, quality of learning is a function of the total curricular and institutional environment in which the students find themselves (Entwistle, 1989).

The teacher–student relationship

First, at the basic level, that of the teacher–student relationship, each teacher bears a heavy responsibility for maintaining and developing the quality of the learning of the students concerned. Perhaps the essential requirement is that each teacher should have a certain degree of humility. Much teaching in further and higher education is surplus to requirements, in two senses: (1) the curriculum tends to be overpacked with material, so that students are obliged to adopt 'surface learning' strategies merely to cope with the flow of experiences and material; and (2) where students are adults – even young adults – there should be a presumption that at least to some extent they can learn by themselves. Teachers need to be able to satisfy themselves that their presence, therefore, actually produces an improved learning experience compared to that which would result in their absence.

Second, each teacher certainly has to have a commitment to his or her subject. But that has to be accompanied by a willingness to work to find ways of producing effective learning experiences for the students. That in turn means trying in part to build a curriculum from the initial perceptions and starting points of the students on entry to the course. Without such an empathy, the teacher's personal commitment to the subject can stand in the way of effective communication.

Third, the teacher has to be conscious of what high quality learning can be, both in general terms and in the context of the cluster of knowledge and skills around which the course is based. The research and development work that has been conducted on learning (touched on above) has been so extensive, both across subjects and at different levels of the education system, that teachers cannot count themselves as full professionals unless they have some understanding of it and have begun to work out its implications for their subject area. Teachers should certainly be trying to promote deep learning in at least some parts of the course; and some kind of holistic view should be gained by the students of their experiences. This is not a prescriptive dogma but a recollection of what education is: a gradual attainment on the part of the student of a position of some independence, whether in the sphere of thought or action. Teachers have to work towards a position of making themselves dispensable, so that their students are able to take up a critical stance for themselves in their chosen field of study or endeavour.

The department

Turning to the second level of institutional action, that of the department, the role of head of department is crucial. The first priority lies in giving signals to the staff which indicate that the quality of their teaching – *in terms of the quality of the students' learning* – matters. That is, the head of department should try to develop a departmental ethos in which a concern for the student experience is high in the department's priorities. Simply providing courses for the students and administering their organization efficiently, including the course assessments, is insufficient. The required ethos needs specific action in order to bring it about. Appropriate actions will vary between subject areas, but the following considerations run across subjects.

First, and most significant, there should be a determination across the department that students are absolutely central to the work of the department, not simply tolerated or endured. This means that their learning, their perceptions, and their rights as learners should be respected. One corollary of this presupposition is that the students should be granted real choices over their learning. The learning needs to be theirs; the students need to be, at least in part, in command of it. We cannot expect higher order levels of learning - of critical thought, of independent judgement, and of identifying and solving significant problems - unless some aspects of the students' learning is under their direction. The pace, the methods, the order, and even parts of the content are all possible candidates for putting at the students' determination. In short, there should be a departmental policy that the curricula on offer will be characterized by a significant degree of open learning.

Staff will need assistance and support in moving in this direction. The staff of the institution's staff development unit will be able to assist, but ultimately on a continuing basis, the best people to help are one's colleagues, who are familiar with the subject matter and are best placed to suggest alternative strategies (Baird, 1988). Staff could be encouraged, by the head of department, to observe each other in action when teaching. The purpose would not be to comment on one's colleague's teaching style as such, but to obtain some insight into the student experience, and so be able to assist in improving that individual's teaching effectiveness. These arrangements should be entirely informal and collaborative, with staff members both observing and being observed. The head of department might initiate them, but should have no part in their organization or conduct, so that the colleagues concerned in no way feel threatened by them.

Ways need to be found, though, of ascertaining student perceptions of their course more systematically. It is now generally recognized that course committees are an unsatisfactory vehicle for this purpose, with a small number of students being put into a relatively exposed position. Many institutions are using student questionnaires on a more or less systematic basis; these have both strengths and weaknesses. The key strength is that, once over the initial design stage, they are relatively economical to administer. The key weakness is that, as with questionnaires generally, they presuppose the issues in which the respondents (here, the students) are interested.

Kingston Polytechnic has adopted a particularly powerful means of eliciting unconstrained student feedback. Acting on invitations from heads of department, a member of the Polytechnic's staff development unit sets up a meeting with the students on a course and engages in a conversation with them, all together, inviting comments on the course.

Negative remarks have to be accompanied by a positive suggestion for improvement. Personal comments on individual members of staff are not recorded. On the basis of the dialogue, a thematically-structured report is made to the head of department who alone decides on subsequent action, if any.

The institution

I turn now to the last level of institutional action to deliver high quality student learning, that of the institution itself. The following are just some ways in which institutions, in their internal management policies, can promote high quality student learning.

Research If an institution is engaged in research, there are two policies it can adopt, complementary to each other. First, it can encourage staff to pursue research which is directly relevant to the curriculum on offer, and to the students' interests. Where there is a culture of research in the institution, staff will often need little prompting of this kind; their teaching motivation is enhanced by their teaching activities being underpinned by their research activities. (Saying this in no way assumes that there is a necessary link between research competence and teaching competence; or that research needs to link at every point to the curriculum.) This matter becomes of managerial interest particularly where an institution possesses little in the way of a research tradition, but recognizes a need to develop in that way, perhaps through undertaking some degree work for the first time. Their teaching effectiveness is surely more likely to be enhanced if their research efforts are linked to some part of the curriculum than if they are not.

Second, staff might be encouraged to undertake research into their own teaching activities. This could be felt to form part of a teacher's professional responsibilities: as a teacher, rather than as a researcher, each teacher should – it might be thought – be interested in evaluating his or her own teaching methods. More to the point here, though, is the related consideration that to gain an informed insight into the quality of the students' learning will require some kind of systematic investigation on the part of the teacher. The teacher cannot assume that the students are generally gaining a deep level of understanding of the material which has been assimilated, or have reached a sceptical, relativistic position, or have gone beyond to a position of personal 'authoritative uncertainty' (Goodlad, 1976, p 84). That knowledge of the students' intellectual development has, in the end, to be grounded in a structured inquiry; and the best-placed person to carry it out is the teacher.

More generally, teaching staff – either by themselves or in collaboration with a central unit in the institution – could conduct research into the student experience. Birmingham Polytechnic, for instance, is testing out a number of evaluation instruments aimed at eliciting the student experience, ranging from a general questionnaire to 'tracking' the students on a class-by-class basis, following their activities through a typical day.

Course review Institutions have a particular opportunity to promote the quality of student learning by ensuring that it is explored in course validation and review. In any such event of any consequence, the course team should be required at the very least to give a statement of their 'philosophy' in relation to the student experience:

- How didactic are staff/student interactions?
- How interactive are lectures?
- What opportunities for independent learning are there?
- Are students encouraged to work in groups?
- Are students required to assess their own work?
- How much initiative are students expected to take in determining their own learning?

The course team ought not simply to present a written statement of this kind, but should be expected to back it up with evidence. The evidence would be determined by the course team; so too, the manner of its presentation. The course leader should, for example, be given the opportunity to present 'in action' and to give the assessors a direct insight into the student experience. This might be permitting members of the review panel to sit in on student seminars; or there might be a demonstration or simulation or performance put on by the students; or there might be a video of a typical series of activities (perhaps showing a site visit by a class or some other staff–student interaction).

For this kind of contribution to course evaluation to be fully useful, at least some members of the course review panel would need to be primed in advance to explore issues of student learning. The general aim would be not to make pronouncements to the course team, but to engage them in discussion so that they can reveal the extent to which they take the quality of their students' learning seriously. It may be that the course team can point to some award for teaching innovation that they have won (whether within the institution or perhaps nationally), or to a new kind of student questionnaire, or to a new method of enhancing the place of work experience within the course. In addition, the review team will wish to balance the staffs' perceptions with those of the students by having a 'private' meeting with a group of the students themselves.

Staff development Staff development is a crucial link in the institution's enhancement of the quality of student learning. There is, at least, a suggestion in the research literature to this effect (Ramsden, 1983; Badley, 1989a). Strangely, though, it is doubtful if – while often extolling their support for staff development – institutions sufficiently orchestrate their staff development activities so that they do lead to more effective learning.

As it is practised, staff development may fulfil at least three different functions. First, it is used to allow teaching staff to gain further qualifications, related to their subject field or to allow them to retrain for a new subject area. Second, it is used to enable staff working in professionally-related areas to gain experience in the working situation or to acquire other related relevant skills. Third, it is used to pump-prime research or consultancy activities. These three main orientations of staff development – for higher qualifications, professional skills and awareness, and research and consultancy – can be represented diagramatically by a triangle: any institution's or department's staff development policies could then be placed at a particular point in the triangular space.

If this is right, there are two problems. First, staff development policies as they are practised are the result of a tacit negotiation between the perceived wants of the institution and the individual staff members. Consequently, they take on something of an *ad hoc* character. Second, on this analysis, using staff development for enhanced teacher effectiveness is played down, and this is hardly surprising since such a use of staff development will seldom be at the top of the agenda of either the institutional management or the teaching staff. Another reason why it may be overlooked is the surprising point that much can be accomplished in this domain relatively inexpensively; it does not require costly year-long staff sabbatical leave. Encouraging self-supportive networks among staff, or running occasional in-house workshops on teaching and learning, does not demand the kinds of resources needed for many of the other kinds of staff development. Consequently, for a staff development committee which sees itself primarily in business to disburse staff development monies, such low-cost activities can easily be neglected.

Institutional ethos

An institution which understands its responsibilities in promoting more effective student learning should have regard to the general institutional ethos. Is it one which accords high priority to student learning and the student experience? Very often, this kind of statement is expressed by institutional managers, but what might it mean in practice? Briefly, the following are just some actions that might be taken at institutional level.

General educational aims In the USA, a number of community colleges (for instance, the Miami-Dade Community College (Badley, 1989b)) have given backing to their claims to take students seriously by identifying – as a collective exercise, across the whole college – a set of specific educational aims that the college wishes to promote. These aims are usually heavily centred on the student experience and the kind of general educational capacities on which the college places a high value. The abilities identified by Alverno College includes effective communication, analytical capability, valuing in a decision-making context, effective social interaction, and taking responsibility for the global environment. In the UK, various national bodies (including the Council for National Academic Awards, BTEC and the former University Grants Committee and the National Advisory Body) have espoused not dissimilar sets of general aims.

The point, though, is that institutions have an opportunity to pick out those capacities that they wish to develop in students in accordance with their own institutional mission. Having identified such a list of valued educational aims, they then need to go on to examine how such a set of aims can be put into practice across the institution. If it has been a genuinely corporate exercise and the ideas have emerged from genuine institutional debate, it should not be too difficult to see that those aims are reflected in the institution's course-evaluation exercises. The Polytechnic of East London, for instance, has underlined its adherence to CNAA's general educational aims by incorporating them explicitly into its own statement on 'Quality', which serves as a set of criteria to be used in the institution's quality assurance exercises (Baume, 1990). But any such institution has to see, if its educational aims are really to become part of the institutional ethos, that they are transmitted and observed by all those having responsibility for the institution's affairs, including external examiners and members of the Board of Governors.

The significance which an institution gives to students, their experience, their development and their emerging capabilities, can come through in other ways, too. Staff appointments and promotions are a vital means of giving the appropriate signals to an institution. Candidates could be asked to demonstrate their commitment to effective teaching, by presenting a portfolio of their past work: it could include handouts, overhead slides, examples of innovative teaching methods, and student questionnaires.

Other means by which an institution's management could help in promoting an ethos conducive to effective learning are:

- Learning week
  In this initiative – now successfully run by several polytechnics – the staff of the whole institution are encouraged to experiment for a week with a completely new teaching method for one of their classes.

- Institutional newsletter
  Many institutions have a newsletter, but how many column inches are given to reporting on teaching and learning? The occasional report of a student having produced an exciting (even an award-winning) project is entirely understandable, but what is really required is a regular report, in some depth, of the way in which a member of staff has designed a successful teaching innovation, written in a non-technical way so that other members of staff can adapt it to different subject areas.
- Teaching awards scheme
  Some institutions have instituted an awards scheme for interesting teaching innovations. The cost to the institution lies not so much in the awards themselves – which can be quite small while still offering an incentive – but in the promotion and organization of the scheme. The assessment of the candidates' submissions, in particular, needs to be handled scrupulously, and to be independent of the Director or Principal.
- Institutional reports
  Easily overlooked is the institution's own documentation, especially that produced for public consumption across the institution and to a wider audience. Precisely because the curriculum constitutes something of 'a secret garden', the institution's other achievements are often much more evident and are more easily reported. Research income, new courses, connections with industry and Europe, and student flows into and out of the institution come readily into view in producing an annual report; but the character of the student experience and the effort being made to enhance student learning must not be forgotten if it is to gain centre stage in the institution's internal life.

Assessing the quality of student learning

I have tried to develop a concept of 'quality' in the context of student learning which is centred around the student's relationship to what has been learnt. Ultimately, what matters is not what the student has learnt, but what the student makes of that learning. Have the students made something of themselves, been enabled to impart and substantiate their own point of view, as well as having a deep understanding of what it is they have encountered? It will be evident from the earlier analysis that assessing the quality of student learning can take place on at least two levels: (1) there is the level of the individual student; and (2) there is the level of the institution's own policies and practices.

We should not assume that, at the level of the individual student, degree classes or grade marks offer a direct insight into the quality of student learning. For that assumption to hold up would depend on the further assumption that examinations always assess the extent to which students have a deep understanding of the material and experiences they have encountered. The fact is that not only has it been possible to pass examinations by the student employing a surface approach to learning; such an approach has often been encouraged by the assessment regime.

We need, therefore, to ensure that the assessment package, in every respect, is designed to encourage a deep learning approach and assesses the student's depth of understanding. This may mean sacrificing some material which students might be expected to show some familiarity with. It also means that the questions and tasks asked of students have to be very carefully designed so that students are required to exercise some independent thought, and have to have a deep understanding of key concepts. This is not to deny that some factual material may have to be mastered, but it is to assert that attention has to be paid to the balance between reproducing such material in a relatively passive form and demonstrating one's ability to use that material in novel situations and possibly to take up a critical stance towards it.

Finally, how might we assess an institution's performance in delivering high quality student learning? This is clearly an important matter if we are concerned about the success of our institutions as *educational* institutions. But it also follows from the treatment offered in this contribution that we cannot easily observe the performance of an institution in this dimension. For what is at stake is what is going on in the minds of our students, and the kind of intellectual development (broadly considered) that they are undergoing. And that has a certain invisibility about it. This means that the current tendency to favour numerical performance indicators as a means of assessing institutional performance has to be treated with extreme scepticism in this particular domain.

Two performance indicators are, on the surface, germane to the issue here: non-completion figures, and data on the pattern of grades of awards. The latter are especially problematic, on technical grounds alone. First, they are, to some degree, context-dependent: they do not provide pure data, but are – to some extent – a function of the historic pattern of classifications or results in the department offering the course in question, and are subject to human intervention. Increasing understanding of national norms, and a belief in the importance of securing funding through (for example) students gaining good degrees, can act as feedback mechanisms governing the examination function. Second, even a high grade is no indication in itself that a student has actually reached the deepest level of understanding of the material and knowledge he or she has encountered. Evidence exists to show that even 'highly able students' will adopt 'surface-atomistic approaches' when faced with certain sets of demands which prompt students to reproduce particular strings of words in their assessments (Ramsden, 1986).

The other performance indicator of possible help in assessing an institution's educational effectiveness is that of non-completion. If we find, for instance, that say 70 per cent of an entry cohort simply is not completing a course, we are entitled to start asking questions about the course. Clearly, learning is unlikely to be of a sufficient quality in that case. But it is, after all, a negative indicator. It can only give us grounds for suspecting that the teaching may not be fully effective, for whatever reason. As a recent acrimonious debate in the pages of the journal *Higher Education* reveals, the actual assessment of non-completion data is highly problematic, for the data reflect a diffuse mix of intervening variables, at teacher, departmental, faculty, institutional and even sector level (Johnes and Taylor, 1990; McPherson and Paterson, 1990).

Numerical performance indicators cannot give us, therefore, even good indications that high quality learning *is* being achieved by an institution as a whole. What we have to do, instead, is look for other kinds of indicator that give us grounds for believing that an institution takes student learning and the student experience seriously. What we need, in short, are indicators that a concern for the quality of student learning is built into the internal life of the institution. In the previous section, I gave some examples of what these might be. If we find an institution which has instituted learning weeks, has a staff development unit concerned about student learning and the student experience, gives tangible rewards for high quality teaching, clearly looks for evidence of a commitment to teaching in its promotions procedures, picks out examples of good teaching in its newsletter, and encourages staff to explore teaching *and* learning intentions within its course review procedures, then we have grounds for believing that here is an institution in which the character of the student experience really matters and is not just a piece of rhetoric.

Conclusion

If, then, we are serious about delivering high quality student learning in academic institutions, we have to do no less than put that at the centre of the institution's culture and mission. Pursuing research, developing links with industry, looking to students' employment prospects, or widening access are all legitimate aims. But unless the individual student, and his or her learning experience is seen by the institution as a whole to constitute the first priority, it is liable to be played down. The problem is that the quality of the student experience, as I have described it here, has little in the way of a constituency pressing its claims (hardly ever the students themselves). Consequently, the other institutional aims, which certainly do have vociferous advocates both inside and outside the institution, come all too easily to take the centre ground. Placing a concern for the student experience, and high quality learning on the part of the student, at the centre of the life of our institution requires, therefore, a paradigm shift in the way in which institutions are managed; for the claims of the largely silent student have to take the centre ground. But even more than that, it requires permanent vigilance if the contending counter-claims for institutional purposes are to be kept in proper balance. A concern for high quality learning is not enough; it has to be fought for, continually, as part of the leadership of an institution.

References

Badley, G (1989a) Excellent teaching in the UK. *British Journal of In-Service Education* 15 (3) 177–86

Badley, G (1989b) *Improving College Teaching and Learning: an American case study.* Anglia Higher Education College (mimeo)

Baird, J R (1988) Quality: what should make Higher Education 'Higher'? *Higher Education Research and Development* 7 (2) 141–52

Baume, D (1990) Defining quality (and using your definition). *Bulletin of Teaching and Learning*, 3, 27–9

Burke, J W (Ed) (1989) *Competency Based Education and Training.* London: Falmer Press

Elton, L (1990) Criteria of excellence in teaching and learning and their appraisal. *Bulletin of Teaching and Learning* 3, 2–5

Entwistle, N (1989) Teaching and the quality of learning in higher education. In N Entwistle (Ed) *Handbook of Educational Ideas and Practices.* London: Routledge and Kegan Paul

Goodlad, S (1976) *Conflict and Consensus in Higher Education.* London: Hodder and Stoughton.

Johnes, J and Taylor J (1990) Undergraduate non-completion rates: a reply. *Higher Education* 19 (3) 385–90

McPherson, A and Paterson, L (1990) Undergraduate non-completion rates: a comment. *Higher Education* 19 (3) 377–83

Marton, F et al (Eds) (1984) *The Experience of Learning.* Edinburgh: Scottish Academic Press

Perry, W G (1970) *Forms of Intellectual and Ethical Development in the College Years.* New York: Holt, Rinehart and Winston

Ramsden, P (1983) Institutional variations in British students' approaches to learning and experiences of teaching. *Higher Education* 12

Ramsden, P (1986) Students and quality. In G Moodie (Ed) *Standards and Criteria in Higher Education.* Milton Keynes: Open University Press

4 Delivering Core Skills 16–19: Implications For Quality

Charles Muir

Introduction

The long-running debate on the 16–19 curriculum reached a significant stage in April 1990 with the publication of the National Curriculum Council's (NCC) advice to the Secretary of State on 'Core Skills 16–19' which he endorsed in principle in his response on 17 May. The School Examinations and Assessment Council (SEAC) was subsequently commissioned by the Secretary of State to look into the implementation and assessment issues surrounding the proposed core and to make recommendations by the end of July 1990. In September 1990 SEAC published a consultative document containing its proposed principles for 'A' and 'AS' Level examinations. That paper underlined the importance of core skills by stating that their assessment should be as rigorous as assessment of other elements of any subject.

The outcome of the national consultation exercise will be publication of the principles in January 1991. SEAC has already stated that further work needs to be done on core skills and on linkage between academic and vocational qualifications. In the meantime it is worth pondering the possible implications of the new development for schools and colleges, in particular how the new core relates to existing initiatives such as the Technical and Vocational Education Initiative Extension Core, what role it will play in opening up routeways between qualifications, and above all how it can improve the quality of what we offer to students in our post-16 institutions and beyond.

At the same time as NCC was publishing its findings the National Council for Vocational Qualifications (NCVQ) produced its Research and Development Paper Number 6, *Common Learning Outcomes: Core Skills in A/AS Levels and NVQs*. It was significant that NCC had consulted a wide range of organizations prior to publication, including NCVQ, the Further Education Unit, and other vocational bodies. Equally important was the fact that, with very few exceptions, the components of the NCC and NCVQ cores showed marked similarities. This will come as no great surprise either to those members of staff in schools and colleges involved over the past few years with the Certificate of Pre-Vocational Education, or to those who have read the report of the Confederation of British Industry, *Towards a Skills Revolution*, published in 1989, which called for greater participation in education and training post-16, a general raising of skills levels and the introduction of what are in effect core skills.

Not only has consensus now been reached across a range of organizations but it is clear that the new core offers a long-awaited opportunity to address the 'academic/vocational divide' issue realistically. It is unlikely that this will be achieved via core skills alone: other linking mechanisms such as 'generic' or 'common' modules will surely find a central place in the new qualifications' structure. Attainment targets and levels in the National Curriculum will need to be linked to post-16 attainments and to National Vocational Qualification levels. Core skills will then become the key that opens doors from one progression route to another. Already the basic tools of learning, they will become the common currency for learners of all ages and abilities, enabling them to gain access to programmes of study which meet their needs and aspirations. The implications reach beyond 'A'/'AS' Levels, beyond the whole range of full-time post-16 vocational qualifications and into the spheres of employment, training and continuing education.

The hallmark of quality in any service is its ability to deliver products tailored to individual needs and tastes and a high standard of customer care: education and training should be no exception. Indeed many institutions, especially in the area of further education, are striving to achieve such a level of provision through assessment on demand, accreditation of prior learning, open and flexible learning packages and student support systems. The move towards a common currency in core skills should make their task much easier by giving a set of benchmarks against which to measure individual attainment in key skill areas.

It is likely that the effects of the proposals will filter through to student programmes by the middle of this decade. Given the impact they will have on the content and style of learning programmes and on guidance and counselling systems, it makes sense for institutions to prepare for them now rather than wait for their imposition at some future date. It is also an appropriate time to widen the dialogue with employers and other users so that all sides are ready for the change.

The core as a concept

The NCC and NCVQ documents not only made the core debate in a sense 'official' but, by stating clearly what the components of the core were and how they might be implemented, offered a useful definition of the concept. It was not to be a 'bolt on' enhancement of a mainstream programme, although certain elements might have to be added to courses where they could not be fully integrated without distorting the teaching/learning experience. It was for this reason that NCC distinguished between a 'primary' skill such as problem solving and a 'second order' skill such as information technology. The first clearly overarches all other skills, and ought to pervade and indeed characterize the whole learning experience of a student. The second, embracing other skills such as problem solving and communication, is a useful context for the acquisition, development and use of those skills, but would not naturally exist in every component of a learning programme. Nor was the proposed core to be a set of 'core' subjects in the National Curriculum pre-16 sense; or a 'core curriculum' as defined in other contexts. The new core was to become the only core, replacing, for example, the core components specific to individual vocational programmes. It was to be integral to every student's programme and 'built in' across the whole range of teaching and learning experiences.

Which core?

There is no doubt that the NCC core, or something very close to it, will become the 'official' core, infiltrating the whole 16–19 curriculum in schools and colleges. However, if it is to play a full role in providing the flexibility demanded by a rapidly changing society it must provide a way into every education or training programme, whether provided in mainstream institutions, via the workplace, or elsewhere. In the meantime curriculum managers, currently attempting to come to terms with its precursors through TVEI Extension, CPVE or other initiatives, may be forgiven if they display a degree of confusion or even, in some quarters, scepticism. While this is understandable it is nevertheless possible to show that the discrepancies between the TVEI and the NCC cores which appear at first sight are mostly a matter of emphasis and 'labelling' rather than of aim and principle. Given the current debate on standards in education and training in this country it is essential that every opportunity is taken to market the new concept to employers and other users.

The Training Agency, in its document *Guidelines for Preparing TVEI Extension Proposals for the 16–18 Phase*, lists a number of Common Learning Outcomes for all 16–18 year olds. It is around these that LEAs, preparing their proposals for the 16–18 phase of TVEI Extension, build their core entitlement for students. According to this all students should be able to:

- Communicate effectively (where possible in more than one language);

- Compile and use numerical information;
- Use science and technology appropriately;
- Understand the world of work;
- Develop effective personal and interpersonal skills;
- Work independently and in teams;
- Solve problems;
- Cope positively with change.

The NCC core concurs with four of these: communication skills, problem solving skills, personal skills and numeracy. However, closer examination of the NCC advice paper reveals further similarities between it and the TVEI Extension version. For, although NCC sees modern language competence as a distinct core component, whereas TVEI see it as a suitable context for the development of communication skills, the NCC requirement that modern language competence should be built into every student programme will ensure that students have access to this key area of learning. As a result both NCC and TVEI Extension criteria will be satisfied. Similarly TVEI Extension's 'Work independently and in teams' and 'Cope positively with change' can be seen as different facets of personal/personal-and-interpersonal skills; and information technology within TVEI Extension would be one of a range of suitable contexts, like modern languages, for the development of communication skills.

Further parallels can be drawn by examining what the NCC paper lists as key themes, or cross-curricular skills. While these are not, strictly speaking, skills but 'areas of awareness' or 'ways of understanding' they are nevertheless vital components in the post-16 learning experience of every individual if there is to be effective progression from the National Curriculum pre-16. They are as follows:

- Economic and industrial understanding;
- Environmental education;
- Education for citizenship;
- Career education and guidance;
- Health education;
- Science and technology;
- Aesthetic and creative understanding.

In addition the NCC document recommends that assignments or projects based in the workplace and in the community should form part of every student's programme and that achievement in core areas across a wide range of contexts, both within and beyond school/college, should be recorded within a single national record of achievement.

All of this brings it even closer to TVEI Extension principles and aims, and into line with the recommendations contained both in the NCVQ paper and the report of the CBI Task Force published in 1989, *Towards a Skills Revolution*.

Table 4.1, in placing the TVEI Extension Common Learning Outcomes alongside the NCC Core Skills and cross-curricular themes, illustrates the extent to which they are running in parallel. It points only to what would appear to be the most obvious links: undoubtedly there will be others.

NCC	*TVEI Extension*
Communication skills	Communicate effectively (where possible in more than one language)
Problem solving skills	All TVEI Extension common learning outcomes
Personal skills	Develop effective personal and interpersonal skills Cope positively with change Work independently and in teams
Numeracy	Compile and use numerical information
Information technology	Communicate effectively (where possible, in more than one language) Solve problems Compile and use numerical information Use science and technology appropriately
Modern language competence	Communicate effectively (where possible in more than one language)
Economic and industrial understanding Work- and community-based projects	Understand the world of work Work independently and in teams
Environmental education Health education Science and technology	Use science and technology appropriately
Education for citizenship Career education and guidance	Develop effective personal and interpersonal skills

Table 4.1 *A comparison of NCC and TVEI Extension Cores*

This last area, Aesthetic and creative understanding, is likely to be the focus of much debate when it comes to planning and implementing the core. For although it will not be difficult to see how it might be offered across a range of student programmes, the resource and time issues may present institutions with problems of a very practical nature. Given the 'basic minimum core' approach taken by a number of TVEI Extension schemes it is not difficult to see why this element is not included in proposals. On the other hand this type of approach acknowledges the need to widen student entitlement when and where possible and is in no way philosophically opposed to the existence, or later introduction of, an aesthetic and creative component.

It can be argued, therefore, that the problem perceived in some areas of assimilating the NCC core to the TVEI Extension and other existing cores is more apparent than real: the real issues lie elsewhere. There can be little doubt that the only way in which core skills and experiences will play their full and proper role in post-16 learning programmes is if their importance and value are fully recognized by all the facilitators of learning as well as by the learners themselves. This will not happen if they are delivered as an adjunct to the 'real' learning programme, as has been the case in some core experiments or viewed as an 'optional extra'. On the contrary the core must be woven into the fabric of every programme.

The role of core skills and experiences

The argument most commonly adduced for the inclusion of core skills and experiences in the curriculum is that they are relevant; they equip young people for the demands of adulthood and working life. The weakness in this argument is, of course, that young people need to acquire and develop those skills for their current needs, since they include very basic learning tools such as problem solving and communication. Once acquired, however, they can be developed to higher levels in different and more demanding contexts. This in turn opens up the possibility for the individual to gain recognition of achievement in the various core skills and take them into new and possibly high level programmes. If we are to achieve the level of client-centred quality provision already discussed it is the responsibility of all providers to ensure that achievement is acknowledged and accredited so that progression routes are truly accessible. The 'relevance' argument, especially in this wider sense, is nevertheless a powerful one, not least where it is seen to address the needs of society. It is the one currently used by those whose chief concerns are the lack of a mobile, flexible workforce in the UK, with a level of skills in the population able to measure up to that of foreign competitors, and the mismatch between the products of our education and training systems and the needs of the workplace.

The attitudes of employers, admissions tutors and other 'consumers' of the products of post-16 education and training are important. Here there is encouragement to be taken from statements emanating from the CBI and other bodies representing the world of business. More employers are looking for evidence of strength in potential employees in general, transferable skills and qualities: application forms are designed to elicit information on much more than the vocationally-specific achievements of young people. There are signs too that higher education is waking up to the possibility that the depth of information contained in a record of achievement may tell them more about an aspiring student and his or her ability to cope with the demands of a university or polytechnic.

There are nevertheless other, arguably more compelling, educational reasons for strengthening the position of core skills and experiences in our post-16 programmes. Among these is the breadth which they can provide, especially within narrowly-focused programmes such as 'A' Levels, and the coherence they can bring to a student's experience of a programme if they are integrated into all aspects of the programme and capable of transfer within it.

Core skills and experiences, if regarded as common learning outcomes for all students, independent of syllabus or course, can in addition provide a more effective way of enabling students to plan and pursue learning programmes which match their specific needs at given stages. Indeed, as has been already suggested, this is one of the hallmarks of a quality provision. It should be possible, once SEAC has completed its work on mapping skills which are common across a range of courses, to build up credit for achievements within specific core areas and transfer them at appropriate points, to another course. This would facilitate progression and transfer not only between courses within one institution but, for example, between different types of courses in separate centres. Core skills and experiences therefore emerge as perhaps the most effective way of 'blurring' the division between the academic and the vocational routes by providing the 'bridges' and 'ladders' long sought after.

Assessing the core

In its investigation into the core in the 16–19 curriculum, SEAC will no doubt listen to the views of a wide range of organizations and institutions. The Secretary of State has asked that it examine ways in which the core might be assessed and what role it should play in the award of grades at 'A' and 'AS' levels. NCVQ has already made its position clear by stating that it assumes that 'core skills will be assessed and their achievement recognized by formal credits'. The NCVQ report goes on to suggest that lessons can be learned from approaches to assessment in both NVQs and the National Curriculum. Clearly, no matter what SEAC ultimately recommends, much work will remain to be done in relating post-16 core achievements to National Curriculum attainments and to NVQ units and elements of competence. Otherwise the credit accumulation and progression and transfer advantages will be lost.

Many of the accreditation issues will have to be resolved and prescribed externally. In the meantime those involved in CPVE and contracted to deliver the core through TVEI Extension will be able to proceed and assimilate the chnges as and when they occur. The 'core in context' approach, familiar to those practitioners, will provide a useful platform of experience on which to build, for it is entirely in line with NCC and SEAC thinking on the subject. What evidence there is on the likelihood of skills transfer suggests that there is a greater chance of it happening where students have been given opportunities to acquire, develop and use skills in as wide a range of contexts as possible.

As far as the assessment of core skills is concerned, schools and colleges already have considerable experience in helping students undertake self-assessment. Anyone who has interviewed CPVE students at the end of their programme and wondered at the confidence they frequently exhibit compared to their peers, need look no further than the review process which, when effectively carried out, encourages the student to reflect on his or her achievements, evaluate them and plan the next stage of learning. It is widely accepted that those elements of any learning programme which allow the student to acquire knowledge, understanding and skills through exploration, problem solving, and practical experience are more effectively learned and more valued where the student has been genuinely at the centre of the learning and assessment process. The advantages which this kind of approach offers in terms of real progression in learning cannot be underestimated. It is this kind of invaluable experience which both students and staff are gaining through programmes such as CPVE and processes such as recording achievement, action planning and negotiating learning contracts. In an institution or system which aspires to quality in its provision the experiences and processes outlined above must be part of the curriculum entitlement of every individual. Moreover, once employers and other users are aware of the skills which potential employees are bringing with them they will be in a better position not only to fit individuals into roles but to match training to needs.

Further development of this nature will have a considerable impact on the way in which schools and colleges deploy their human resources and plan and allocate their use of time. The task of the tutor in helping students assemble and evaluate evidence of attainment will call for thorough staff training in the appropriate skills involved in this process as well as a fresh look at the role and status of those individuals within institutions. The job of dealing with the learning needs of young people arriving on the threshold of post-16 education and training with a complex array of attainments in the National Curriculum pre-16, will call for a high level of skills, realistic time allocation, and employer involvement.

The next few years

It is fairly obvious that the wise strategy is not to wait and see what emerges from SEAC and elsewhere but to build on the considerable development already taking place through TVEI Extension and other initiatives. The pool of expertise built up as a result of CPVE has also been mentioned; added to that is the widespread experience in the vocational sector in teaching and assessing core skills. Currently many institutions are seriously addressing the issue of core in student programmes under the auspices of TVEI Extension by using the process of curriculum audit to identify areas where core skills exist, or otherwise. Individual student programmes can then be planned accordingly. Therefore, while it is almost inevitable that, for example, 'A' Level syllabuses will be changed in the next three to four years to accommodate the core, institutions still need to continue with their development work in this area. This will enable individual members of staff to become gradually familiarized with the new approach to core and its implications for planning and managing the learning experiences of their students, and assessing the outcomes of that experience.

Above all, if the core stands any chance of success it will be through a process of evolutionary change rather than in a 'giant leap'. In this context the NCVQ research and development paper already referred to issues a timely note of caution. Referring to the task of building-in a core to learning programmes and the attendant management and staff development implications, it states:

> The recent history of curriculum development and innovation is littered with failures. Many of these initiatives, which were well-researched and well-resourced, failed at the point of implementation. Reasons for failure were various; what many failures had in common was an inability to 'embed' themselves in existing good practice.

In managing the changes brought about by the introduction of the core across the post-16 spectrum curriculum managers will do well to heed this advice. When members of staff claim, often with some justification, that they have been teaching core skills for years, they need to be regarded, not as an obstacle to be circumvented, but as an invaluable resource which has to be harnessed and nurtured.

Conclusion

Concern with quality rightly dominates much of our discussion these days when it comes to educational matters. But how shall we recognize quality when we see it? Surely the answer lies in a system of provision which recognizes that education is a lifelong process, that learning takes place in a wide variety of contexts and that it is the responsibility of the providers to ensure that each individual has a right to develop his or her skills and personal qualities to their true potential. Such a system must be able to bend, to meet the learner on his or her own terms and provide the resources and support appropriate to his or her individual needs.

Are core skills the answer? They are, but only within the constraints of a qualifications structure which is imperfect and is likely to remain so long after the dust has settled on the SEAC principles document. If the map of education and training in the future is to look more like a well signposted motorway than a complex and bewildering maze, boldness and imagination are needed, not occasional 'tinkering' with what we already have. On the way to a simpler, more comprehensible system of qualifications a few well-loved brand names may have to be discontinued, but that would be a small price to pay for meeting the developmental needs of individual learners. In the National Curriculum we have the basis for a broad programme of learning and assessment within which individuals can progress within a single qualification framework at a pace and to a level in keeping with their abilities, needs and aspirations. Is it too much to expect the extension of this facility beyond the age of 16?

5 Quality in Higher Education: The Independent Study Experience

Eunice Hinds

Fundamental to the notion of independent study is 'student centredness': it follows that for this form of education quality is primarily concerned with meeting the needs of the individual student. These needs are met within the framework of approved awards and span the Diploma in Higher Education (Dip HE), graduate and postgraduate work but it is not necessarily within the context of existing subject boundaries.

The term 'independent study' has created problems over the years but attempts to find a better description have not been successful. The study is 'independent' in that it is not limited by subject area and is designed by the student. It is not 'independent' of all restrictions because there are course regulations and a recognized level must be obtained. There is a clear affinity to the idea that what is happening is 'experiential learning' but as Weil and McGill (1989) have pointed out, this is not a universally agreed term. They define four 'villages' and I would locate the School for Independent Study (SIS), in the village which they describe as 'Village Two: experiential learning and change in higher and continuing education', but it is quite possible that other colleagues would perceive the School differently. This has been an on-going debate within the School.

'Experiential' is not seen by the School as preferable to 'independent'. Other possibilities include 'student centred learning', 'self-managed learning', 'contract learning', 'negotiated learning' and 'learner-managed learning'. All these terms have their own problems. The School has recently organized a conference which adopted the term 'learner-managed learning' but only by giving a list of possible meanings for this term.

Finding the term to describe 'independent study' is difficult, as is describing the process to people (students or fellow academics) who are only familiar with traditional teaching methods. The students who go through the process plan their own course, take responsibility for implementing it and finally present their work for assessment, which includes a critical review. In more traditional academic courses tutors plan the 'curriculum' whereas in independent study the tutors plan the process and the facilitative support provided but the students identify their own objectives, specify the output and design the specific learning process.

The school has had 15 years experience of independent study. Over 1,000 students each year experience the process at Diploma, Degree or Postgraduate level. Over the years the course design has changed but the fundamental process remains the same.

History

The School was founded in 1974. The James Report on teacher education in England and Wales (1972) had recommended that the first two years of training should be general education, with the teaching specialism only starting in year three. This was planned to give students the opportunity to make the commitment to a teaching vocation layer. The Dip HE was established as a nationally recognized award which could be either a terminal qualification or the first part of a teaching qualification. The first Dip HE course to be validated by the Council for National Academic Awards was at the North East London Polytechnic (NELP).

In designing the course the academics from NELP had talked to the teaching profession but also to industry and other professions. The overwhelming message was that a 'general competence' course was needed rather than a course which would teach particular subject knowledge. There was an awareness of rapidly changing requirements in all fields of employment as well as the changes in both the particular skills required for any job and the types of jobs which were likely to be available in the future. Against this background the decision was made that the NELP course would be a skills-based course. These skills would not be subject specific: students would learn how to find and use information rather than learning information.

As Bradbury et al (1982) note:

> The Dip HE's aim was to enable people to become educated without necessarily having to accept an established body of knowledge. It was felt that the student's expert knowledge in one field should be balanced by an ability to work in other areas. The planning team became increasingly aware that employment opportunities change so there is a need to adapt and modify skills. The notion of 'general competence' developed and it became an aim of the course to ensure that all students had what came to be termed 'transferable skills'.
>
> In order to allow students to work on acquiring skills which would be transferable to different situations, not just relevant to a special interest, the idea of central studies

> developed. The aim of a central studies component was to allow students to learn appropriate transferable skills and knowledge ... through workshops and similar activities and further to use these skills by working with peers. Thus developed, the notion of group project work, where groups of students themselves identify problems and then work on solving them . . . collaborating with others, therefore, came to be seen as an aim of the Dip HE, and it was hoped the students would develop interpersonal skills (p 52).

The polytechnics had been set up under a Labour government with the aim of expanding education. The Polytechnic of East London (PEL), which NELP became in 1989, is situated in a poor area of London where the 'take up' rate for Higher Education is very low. The School for Independent Study aimed to increase this for the local population and to use project work to serve the community in which it was situated. The desire to increase access led to admitting students on the basis of their previous experience rather than relying on traditional examination passes.

The need to offer progression for the first cohort of students to enable students to continue their education led to the Degree by Independent Study being established in 1976 and the Postgraduate Diploma/Masters Degree in 1984. The School has grown from one programme of 73 full-time students (1971) to three programmes of 1,000 students (both full-time and part time) each year and from the East End of London its activities now span the globe.

Educational philosophy

'All education planning and organisation should start from the individual student. Whatever is done must be best for him', wrote Tyrrell Burgess (1977), the first Head of the SIS. All the programmes of the School give power to the students; the courses are those of the individual students. The learning process is central and the content is supportive, the students initiate and take responsibility for the formulation of problems, testing tentative solutions to hypotheses, and evaluating the outcome.

The School does not provide courses: instead it provides a recognized framework within which the students can design their own courses. These courses start where the student is, go where the student wants to go and finish at the student's own identified target. They are therefore relevant in a way that no course designed by academics can be. The staff of the School do not teach, rather they allow the students to learn. Socrates would probably have recognized the method more easily than most twentieth century academics. The ideas of Karl Popper (1959–76) influenced the design of the Dip HE and have continued to be a basis for work within the School. For Popper the first stage is the formulation of a problem: in the School students are helped to formulate their own educational problem.

The second stage is to propose possible solutions: this is the student's course plan. The third stage is to test: Popper argues that a scientific statement is one that can be falsified, not verified, because no amount of verification can confirm the truth while one falsification proves the error. The operation of the student's course is the testing and may involve reformulation of the problem or looking for alternative solutions in the light of evidence.

George Klemp (1977) argues that subject knowledge, *per se*, is not a deciding factor in occupational success. He claims there are three factors affecting success:

- the cognitive skills that are exercised and developed in the process of knowledge acquisition and use;
- interpersonal skills, particularly accurate empathy and the ability to promote feeling of efficacy in another person;
- motivation, which involves identifying and meeting one's own targets, taking risks and using interpersonal skills.

The emphasis needs to be on learning how to cope and how to keep up with change. Factual knowledge will, in the modern world, soon become obsolete. There is no point in increasing the number of facts learnt; a much more participative approach to education is needed.

The Royal Society of Arts recognizes this need in its 'Education for Capability Awards'. One of the first such awards given to Higher Education went to the SIS. The Confederation of British Industry has called for personal qualities such as motivation, ability for original thought, and the ability to get at and solve real problems as the product of education. These are just the abilities which the School's students develop. There have now been more than 2,000 students through the School and there have been over 2,000 different courses: each one of those students was motivated to solve a real problem – their own educational design was the proposed solution.

The method

The three programmes of study involve the same processes: admissions, planning, registration, monitoring and final assessment.

Admissions For the Dip HE students are interviewed in groups and offered places if they understand the course, are motivated and are likely to benefit. Previous experience is taken into account so qualifications are not essential. Many students come to the course from 'access' courses or community involvement of some sort. On the Degree and Postgraduate course appropriate level qualifications are required, although exceptions are made for people with appropriate experience at an advanced level. For the Degree and Postgraduate courses admission is to 'free standing' planning courses and students only actually join the course itself on registration.

Planning For the Dip HE this takes place during the first one or two terms of the course. On the other courses it is a one-term free-standing course. All students identify a specialist field in which they wish to work and negotiate support from a tutor who is an expert. Most of these expert tutors are from other areas of the Polytechnic but occasionally outside help is brought in. In the plan the student basically considers:

- Where have I been and where am I now?
- Where do I want to go?
- How do I get from A to B?
- How do I know I have arrived?

Planning is not just a means of setting out a programme of study, or selecting modules. It is a valuable learning experience. When the student asks 'Where have I been and where am I now?' a realistic assessment of experience, strengths and weaknesses is required. This is a way of establishing the value of prior experience.

In the same way a realistic assessment of long term goals (personal, educational and vocational) is required by the question 'Where do I want to go?' The fact that the course is built on the student's own answer to this question means that the commitment is high. Once a general answer to 'How do I get there?' has been given the student is able to negotiate the details with an expert. The student then defines the final point of achievement (dissertations, examinations, exhibitions, projects); the criteria of judgement are also required.

Basically during the planning period the student draws up a 'learning contract'. This is a negotiated document which is founded on the CNAA agreed course objectives and procedures. The student will have negotiated a specialist programme with a tutor who will supervize this study and possibly provide 'placements' where work experience or similar activities will take place. There will also be supporting workshops and other activities.

Registration For the Degree and Postgraduate course there is a Registration Board which considers the proposals. This Board includes external examiners. The proposal must be registered before the student can enrol on the course. For the Dip HE there is a Validating Board which considers the School's judgement on 'statements' of students. This Board is a group of eminent people who verify the standard of the work being undertaken on the course. These Boards signify the School's acceptance of the 'contract' as negotiated by the student. Any student who does not have a supported 'statement' after two terms (full time) is not allowed to continue on the course.

Assessment For the Dip HE students need to satisfy the requirement of 'diligence and attendance' at the end of their first year. On the Degree course it is usual for students to submit course work as part of their final assessment. Personal Tutor Groups are used in all programmes as a way of helping students monitor their own progress.

Final assessment of the specialist subject is done internally by the supervisor and a disinterested person. The results are available for the external examiners' comments. The external examiners are experienced in marking of a comparable level. They are asked to verify that, given the distinctive nature of the course and the criteria as valid, the work is of a level appropriate to the award. It is noticeable that at Honours Degree level the number of First Class awards is high in comparison with most courses. The School considers this is probably caused by the dual factors of exceptionally high motivation and the originality of project.

Liaison This is both with other faculties within the Polytechnic and externally. Within the Polytechnic the main function of liaison is the placement of students with experts in their field of interest. One of the main advantages of working at the Polytechnic rather than the student studying entirely alone is this access to tutors.

Outside the Polytechnic there are two functions of liaison. The first is the obtaining of recognition for the School, which includes placement of students when appropriate, acceptance of the qualifications and sponsorship of students. The second is to re-educate the educators. This is an ambitious aim, but people are fascinated to hear of our experience. They are genuinely interested in what we are doing. They see the advantages and the opportunities although they sometimes lack the courage to try, often because of institutional inertia.

Learning contracts

As will be seen from the above section on planning, all students write their own 'learning contract'. This is relatively new terminology within SIS and is only used on the Dip HE. Until 1988 students wrote 'statements' on the Dip HE, and they still write 'proposals' on the Degree and Postgraduate Courses. Writing these documents involves the students in evaluating their background, assessing their strengths and weaknesses, their academic background and their competence for the course of study they are proposing. Each document is as individual as the student who writes it and each student brings a unique set of personal circumstances, competences and qualifications on which to base the proposal for a programme of study.

The Dip HE document tends to concentrate more on the skills, strengths and weakness and the personal experience, while the Degree and Postgraduate documents are more qualifications-based. It is, however, true that for all programmes the planning of the course must start with the student's own background. The document then identifies the student's aim in terms of personal, educational and vocational outcomes of the course. Students define the objectives of their study and propose ways of obtaining these objectives. There is also a suggestion of how assessment can ensure that these objectives have been met.

This emerging document is basically designed by the student but there is considerable help, support and suggestion from both a personal and specialist tutor. Essentially, this is a negotiation process and like all negotiations the specifics will depend on what is being negotiated and the personalities involved. The final document is put forward for validation (Dip HE) or registration (Degree and Masters) and at this point becomes a contract in the sense that the student agrees to do the work, the tutor to supervize and the Polytechnic to provide the resources.

The student experience

The SIS is now the second largest department in the Polytechnic and supplies students to all other departments. Many tutors who supervize independent study projects find that there are tremendous advantages. The most obvious benefit is the professional updating which inevitably takes place when one is involved with original project work. Some tutors and students have produced joint research. Occasionally students assist with existing research projects being undertaken by tutors in order to improve their skills, for example in statistical analysis. Within the School itself members of staff act as both 'central tutor' (this is a personal tutoring role which assists with the planning and monitoring of the student's programme and ultimately co-ordinates the assessment) and as the 'expert' tutor for students studying within their area of expertise. The staff have a very wide variety of backgrounds and subject expertise. The one thing they all have in common is their enthusiasm for this method of study.

There are, obviously, a wide and interesting variety of student projects at all levels of independent study. The following is a sample list of recent project titles at each of the three award-bearing levels.

- *Diploma of Higher Education*
  - Stress and Women Managers;
  - The Impact on the Stock Exchange of 'the Big Bang';
  - Decision-making in the European Economic Community;
  - A Critical Look at English Literature;
  - Family Counselling in the West Indian Community;
  - Alternative Financing of the National Health Service;
  - How to Start a Small Business.
- *Degree (BA or BSc)*
  - Subsistence Farming: a Comparison of Indian and Highland Crofting;
  - Can Management Practice developed in Large Industry Transfer to Small Business in Less Developed Countries?
  - Accessories for 'Street Wise' Fashion;
  - The Potential for Life Insurance in Nigeria;
  - Lasers and Holograms;
  - Russian Science Fiction.
- *Masters MA or MSc*
  - A Management Training Scheme for Primary Health Workers in Pakistan;
  - A Comparison of the Rehabilitation of Prisoners in Sweden and the United Kingdom;
  - 'Project Full Employ': an Assessment of the Work of the Manpower Services Commission;
  - Advertising Britain in China;
  - Osteopathic Treatment of Foot Complaints;
  - Satellite Surveying Methods.

This list shows not only the wide variety of projects but also the international dimension to the work of the School. Some of the projects with international titles are being carried out by students who may have originated in the country concerned but are now permanently resident in Britain (eg Life Insurance in Nigeria). A number of projects have been carried out by overseas students and include study in London or 'distance learning'.

Student destinations

Probably the greatest vote of confidence in the work of the School is that we now employ several of our own graduates. These come from a variety of traditional study fields so a brief look at their histories probably serves to indicate the diversity both of staff and students.

One ex-student who joined the staff has since moved on. An Austrian resident in the UK, she originally worked in brewery management but after becoming alcoholic took treatment and then looked for a change of career. She did the Dip HE working on textile design and then her degree specialism was print on fabric for the fashion industry before joining the staff on a temporary contract. After two years in the School she decided, for personal reasons, to move to America and work freelance.

The one permanent member of staff who is an ex-student started as a hairdresser with no academic qualifications. When her son was taking his GCE examinations she went to evening classes so that she could help him with his maths. She became so enthusiastic about adult education that she came to the School to do a Dip HE looking at teaching methods for adults. She then did the Independent Study Degree looking at educational management and followed this by a Postgraduate teaching qualification at another college. At this point she was offered a temporary contract. This contract is now permanent and she is also Honorary Secretary of the World Education Fellowship (WEF).

A Sri Lankan who had done three years on a standard university course before coming to study at the School is now working as a half-time temporary lecturer with the School. Coming from a wealthy doctor's family in Sri Lanka and being public school educated, a medical course seemed the natural choice. However, dissatisfaction with the prevailing attitude to medicine led him to seek an alternative. Because of his previous study he was able to go straight on to a Degree pre-course where he planned a programme of study which looked at alternative medicine. After graduating he started consultancy work at an alternative medical centre and he is still working there part-time as well as in the School.

As can be seen from the above profiles several of our students have experience of more traditional education before or after their Independent Study. All of them prefer the independent study model. Those who have gone on to other courses after independent study found the standard method of teaching far less stretching. These profiles of some of our students who have become members of the staff of the School, illustrate the other activities in which they are engaged: as can be seen these include freelance design and alternative medical consultancy. From the brief 'histories' above it can be seen that a number of students from the School go on to other courses.

Many of the School's students have gone into teaching. This can be achieved by completing the Degree and then studying for a Postgraduate Certificate or by doing the Dip HE and then doing a two-year course leading to a BEd. Given that the Dip HE originally started as a result of a review of teacher training (The James Report, 1972) it is logical that this should be the goal for many students.

Social work in some form attracts a large number of independent study students. As has been pointed out many of the School's students come from deprived backgrounds and the wish to return and serve their community is often strong. Probation officers, social workers and community workers are numbered among our ex-students.

A fairly large proportion of former students (between 25 and 30 per cent) become freelancers or start their own business. This is considerably higher than on more traditional courses and is probably the result of the teaching method which fosters an attitude of self-reliance. It can, however, be argued that those who are attracted to an independent study course have an entrepreneurial personality. Examples of the sort of businesses vary from a highly successful safety consultancy for the North Sea Oil industry to a freelance photographer by way of a fish farmer!

Sometimes the staff are surprised when a former student hits the headlines and the circumstances reveal the level of attainment. Such was the situation when the national press, in reporting the aftermath of the Zeebrugge ferry disaster, told the story of a bereavement counsellor who was called in to help the relatives. She was a former student of the SIS. Her problem, identified on joining the Dip HE, was to come to terms with her own loss. She moved on through the degree by independent study to learn counselling skills so that she could help others in similar positions. Her success was demonstrated in a very tangible form.

International links and future developments

The School has established an international reputation. It is active in the World Education Fellowship, publishes *INIS* (*The International Newsletter for Independent Study*), provided much of the impetus for the first International Conference on Experimental Learning in London in 1987, and is often asked to give presentations at international venues.

In April 1990 the School was joint host (with the WEF and Royal Society of Arts) to the First International Learner Managed Learning Conference. The conference has led to the publication of a *Network Directory* for people involved in this form of education.

Recently the idea of franchising the process has become established. After a period of staff development and a validation visit from the PEL, Suffolk College started franchising the Dip HE in October 1989 and the Degree in October 1990 (Pre-course started in April 1990). Other colleges are also negotiating to franchise all or part of courses.

Future developments include a new Certificate in Planning for Professional Development by Independent Study. This will partly be used by staff in Education who wish to develop their expertise in this process of independent study with a view to using it in their own practice.

It is clear that the School for Independent Study in the newly renamed Polytechnic of East London, is thriving and delivering quality education to an increasingly large and diverse student population.

References

Bradbury, P, Hinds, E, Humm, M and Robbins, D (1982) Innovation in independent study at NELP. In D Teather (Ed) *Towards the Community University*. London: Kogan Page

Burgess, T (1977) *Education After School*. Harmondsworth: Penguin

James (1972) *Teacher Education and Training* (The James Report). London: HMSO

Klemp, G (1977) *Three Factors of Success in the World of Work*. New York: Boston McBer

Popper, K (1959) *The Logic of Scientific Discovery*. London: Hutchinson

Popper, K (1976) *The Unintended Quest: An Intellectual Autobiography*. London: Fontana

Weil, S and McGill, I (1989) *Making Sense of Experiential Learning*. Milton Keynes; Open University and Society for Research into Higher Education

PART III

Quality: Employers as Clients

The three chapters in Part III explore from different perspectives the perceptions and roles which employers have in relation to vocational education and training. There is no doubt that employers are major customers of the education and training service. There is a clear, definable need for a trained and educated workforce and to a considerable degree the opportunities for students to study and gain skills are determined by the availability of jobs. Industry, commerce and the professions have argued strongly for strengthening the links between education and employers and recent government policy has built on this. It must be remembered, of course, that the main aim of industry and commerce is to ensure profitable trading, and consequently future employees are seen as critical components in the production process. Nevertheless, it must also be recognized that the public sector remains a major corporate employer across the UK and it is necessary that educational providers satisfy the needs of both private and public sector organizations.

The role of employers in the education and training process has taken on major importance following the recent Education Reform Act (1988). This Act has encouraged employers to become more involved by taking greater responsibility in both the school system and in post-16 education. Employers are now in a majority on the governing bodies of institutions of further and higher education. This has resulted in there being fewer representatives of the public sector and, in particular, of Local Authorities. The establishment of Training and Enterprise Councils, through which significant funding will be available for post-16 vocational education, has placed considerable responsibilities on employers in identifying local employment needs and in contracting educational providers to satisfy them. These government initiatives complement the existing framework, in which employers have played a significant role in vocational education through participating on course management committees, employer consultative groups, and in undertaking teaching and examining. So while there is a clear political shift further to involve employers in vocational education, there is an argument which suggests that this is a means of formalizing those links which already exist. Certainly, such links extend to both private and public sector employers and it would appear that government bodies and Training and Enterprise Councils (TECs) are ensuring representation from both sectors.

There is no doubt, however, that in resourcing employer-led bodies a greater onus will be placed on educational providers, not only to satisfy the immediate needs of their students but to ensure that employers themselves are satisfied by the quality of the product. This theme is explored in Chapter 6, where Bax, in discussion with Dave Müller, explores the role of TECs in ensuring the quality of vocational education. Bax suggests that in order to evaluate fully the effectiveness of vocational education, there is a need to undertake what he refers to as 'impact' studies. By this he means that students should be followed up systematically in the workplace to see the impact they have both in the short term and over a period of time on the organization in which they are working. This goes beyond the traditional monitoring data collected by external funding bodies, who rarely follow up sensitively the ways in which the products of the educational system influence private and public sector employer organizations. There is a very strong case for the TECs to build on the impressive work undertaken by the Manpower Services Commission in monitoring and evaluating educational provision by undertaking more qualitative and long-term follow-up studies.

Bax also offers a number of interesting perceptions on the different approaches to evaluating quality offered through BS 5750 and the broader perspective of 'Total Quality Management'. These issues have been explored in Chapters 1 and 2 and what would seem to be emerging is a consensus that the introduction of BS 5750 and ISO 9000 is a step along the line towards ensuring quality, but is not in itself sufficient to maintain it. Consequently and in line with many major educational providers, a number of the TECs are exploring the possibility of introducing total quality procedures internally. The implication of this is that they are likely to be looking to providers of vocational education to implement similar approaches. It is worth noting that at the same time as TECs and educational providers are exploring total quality management, the same themes and issues are being taken up by industry and a number of public sector organizations. There is clearly considerable opportunity here for industry to work alongside educational providers in exploring the implications of implementing a total quality approach to ensure standards. This strengthens the argument put forward by Bax, that employers, educational providers and students should be working together towards a shared understanding of the role of vocational education and the development of appropriate standards.

Another interesting theme which emerges from the interview with Bax is the emphasis he places on broadening the curriculum. The need for breadth as well as the development of occupational specific competences has been explored in Chapter 3. The same themes seem to be emerging simultaneously from both employer representatives and educationalists. The promotion of core skills beyond the age of 16 is in line with the argument that the development of the individual is more important than the immediate knowledge and skills acquired through education. A different way of looking at this is in terms of the emphasis currently being placed on the development of entrepreneurial skills and the extent to which they enable individuals to respond flexibly to changing work environments. This is not to decry the need for subject specialist competences, but to pinpoint a major role for education in ensuring that students themselves are developed as individuals within the context of a broad occupational framework.

This theme has been reinforced by a recent paper published by the Council for National Academic Awards on the role of higher education in preparing people for work (Boys et al, 1989). This paper notes that higher education leads to a wide range of identifiable skills, including those relating to the discipline, those relating more broadly to communication and teamwork, and those to specific areas of application. At the same time it would appear that many tutors working in subject-specific areas such as Business Studies, Engineering, and the Humanities, are of the view that study within these areas leads to the development of a wide range of transferable skills. Boys et al recommend that institutions could benefit from a review of the extent to which tutors ensure that all students in higher education develop the following transferable qualities:

- to be able to express themselves adequately both orally and in writing;
- to be able to work in groups, seminars, workshops and laboratories in teams as well as individually;
- to have a working knowledge of elementary information technology; and to have some awareness of the relationship of their subject to the wider concerns of the economy and society (p 17).

It is particularly fascinating that the core curriculum debate has spread from its implementation within compulsory education, to the development of personal qualities beyond the age of 16 into that now formally designated as higher education. This will clearly be one of the major themes which relates employer needs to vocational education during the next decade.

Another aspect of delivering quality vocational education is explored in the case study by Barry (see Chapter 7). He describes a consultancy undertaken by Cardiff Institute of Higher Education in which a Medical Laboratories Science course was tailor-made for a client group in the United Arab Emirates. Such consultancies are relatively common in further and higher education and bring together the expertise of educational providers with the occupational needs of employer groups. This case study illustrates how an entrepreneurial culture in vocational education can benefit prospective employers and generate additional income.

The two case studies presented in Chapters 7 and 8 illustrate the ways in which the links between education and employers are developing. The short case study by Hind (see Chapter 8) is an excellent illustration of how, at tutor level, a Degree course in Business Studies can, in partnership with a local firm, explore curriculum issues to the benefit of both students and employers. The enormous amount of preparation in facilitating this kind of initiative must not be underrated, but at the same time it demonstrates clearly how on a course-by-course-basis it is possible to establish purposeful and meaningful links between education and industry.

Does the learner benefit from greater employer involvement in vocational education? There is a paradox worthy of exploration here. It is clear that young people are being encouraged through the development of core generic skills to become more entrepreneurial and to take greater responsibility in negotiating future employment. This is partly in response to the demands employers have made upon the educational system. At the same time demographic trends indicate that there will be many fewer young people entering the workforce during the next five years, while the implications of the Single European Market will increase mobility among the younger workers (see Funnell and Müller, 1991). In partnership with employers, the educational process is working to develop a new range of competences and capabilities in young people. Essentially the process is empowering students and putting them in a position to be selective in terms of future work opportunities. Paradoxically this makes it more difficult for employers to be certain that their involvement in the educational system will be of immediate benefit to them, particularly as the options open to young people become wider as scarcity makes them more valuable commodities.

The paradox is, then, that while employer involvement in the educational process can be seen as being of significant benefit to those in education and training, it does not necessarily lead to meeting the immediate needs of employers themselves and meeting existing skills shortages. The partnership referred to by Bax must be one in which not only is education influenced by employers, but employers themselves review their own work practices and potential role in facilitating continuing education and training. Partnerships by definition are symbiotic and the ways in which education influences employers are as important as the ways in which employers influence education.

References

Boys, C, Brennan, J, Henkel, Kirkland, M, Kogan, M and Youll, P (1989) *Higher Education and the Preparation for Work*. London: CNAA

Funnell, P and Müller, D J (1991) *Vocational Education and the Challenge of Europe*. London: Kogan Page

6 Promoting Quality and Economic Development: The Role of Training and Enterprise Councils (TECs)

Mike Bax
in conversation with Dave Müller

DM: Tell me, Mike, what do you consider to be the role of TECs in promoting quality in vocational and educational training?

MB: There are two sides to the TECs, aren't there? The first is ensuring that what the TEC itself delivers meets certain levels of quality; and the other side is influencing what others are doing, particularly employers. Across those two, I think the TEC has a major responsibility for articulating debates about what quality actually is and how it is best achieved. One particularly interesting development which I think will be coming up in the not too distant future, will be the 'Investors in People Awards', being developed by the National Training Task Force. It will be helpful for TECs to pick up this national initiative and promote it locally to encourage interest from employers. I am sure this will be one of the major initiatives which the TEC strategy will be built around.

DM: What responsibilities do you believe employers have in terms of promoting quality?

MB: In many cases employers do see education and training to be occupation-specific, and I think there is a debate to be encouraged to broaden this view and to encourage, for example, recognition of the importance of interpersonal skills and the approach to change.

DM: If I were asking you to identify priorities, would developing a more generic approach to education and training be one of them – if not the main one?

MB: I certainly think it is *one* of the priorities, and many people are, for example, concerned about some of the NVQ's coming out at the moment which are considered to be rather too specific. I think it is important to preserve the broad-based nature of Youth Training because the broader the range of skills young people have, the more flexible the workforce will be in the future. And, I think that this must be an important aspect of the debate.

DM: If I take this one stage further, can I ask what you judge to be the major requirements, and therefore planned outcomes, of vocational education and training, bearing in mind the need to deliver quality? Really, I'm asking for your views, or a vision, of where we are trying to go.

MB: That's the 64,000 dollar question, isn't it? Clearly, you're right to emphasize outcomes, and we can look around to see what evidence is available on which we can make our judgements or predictions. We can obviously do things like record the attainment of vocational qualifications, or entry into jobs, and we can evaluate the skills in relationship to those jobs. We can look at things like price of the products. We can look at it in terms of flexibility and mode of delivery and there do exist measures of these kinds of things, or at least crude proxies.

I think, however, the much more interesting debate on quality involves looking at the impact of training first and foremost on employers who use the young people or adults from the courses we run, and the degree to which individuals apply those skills immediately and subsequently in the things they do. This is an area which I think the TEC has to become involved in through its different evaluation strategies, although there is no established practice around at the moment to help us.

DM: I find that very interesting personally because you seem to be arguing that the efficiency models which tend to focus on monitoring data, such as the number of students successfully completing a course, are insufficient criteria by which to judge quality, but can be seen as one of the steps on the way to attaining it. I agree with your view that we should start the debate at the other end, that is, on the impact of what we do on our customers, our customers being employers and individuals. The question is, how do individuals utilize, develop and apply these skills? – which I think takes us into an area which we must become involved with.

MB: This involves undertaking employer studies, possibly on a sample basis. I would think as well that it would have to be on an annual cycle and I'm not entirely clear in my own mind yet whether we should sample the same employers over a period of years, or sample different employers on an annual basis.

DM: You really are talking about a different level of analysis which is much more qualitative and which is much more sensitive.

MB: Yes, absolutely. We can all make judgements on the basis of the evaluation measurements we currently have available, but do we know, for example, whether or not we are offering the right products? I suppose that would be the ultimate determinant of quality. Does the training and education input we provide actually coincide with the needs of those individuals and the needs of those employers that employ them? And, I have a feeling that we may find some areas of mismatch.

DM: How far along the line would you go then, in arguing that we have got an outcome model of education and training which is very much based on clearly identifiable outputs such as Level 2 NVQ, or a specific competence? There has been a debate in education for some time emphasizing the fact that education and training is actually a process of getting people to be able to think through issues, become interpersonally skilled problem solvers, able to use the products they have acquired? This does, I think, lead much more towards your impact study in that it focuses on what happens in practice, rather than simply on the product outcomes of education and training.

MB: Yes, it is very clear that there is no consensus as I have been able to detect it, and I have heard some people argue that quality is very much about qualifications and standards, which include of course specific skills. I have heard others argue that, as long as you make sure standards are consistently applied, it doesn't matter in which discipline you train, in that you will acquire generic as well as occupational specific skills. I am not that sure, however, that these common standards do exist if you consider, for example, the differing times needed to complete NVQs of the same level. Certainly, it is important that the individual has demonstrated the ability to learn and actually has a basis for transfer from one industry to another industry if he or she chooses to do so.

DM: So the model of quality is delivering transferable, flexible skills?

MB: I think one thing that schemes like YTS have established over the years is that there is an overwhelming argument for maintaining breadth of development in the two important years between the ages of 16 and 18, but at the same time undertaking a programme which increasingly sharpens up occupational interests and aspirations, and provides those skills which are in line with perceived directions. I'm sure that is right, although some employers and individuals may argue differently; why I believe we must do much more to assess the effectiveness in terms of the utilization of those skills and those personal qualities in the workplace subsequently.

DM: The proposed 16-plus core curriculum will obviously have a major impact on this. What are your views?

MB: Yes. I'm sure in order to meet the needs of industry, for many young people the core curriculum will have to be enhanced with occupational skills as well. I tend to speak as one of those who is not strongly in the occupational camp, nor the generic skills camp. I rather believe that most young people and employers are expecting something between the two, although I guess that to some extent this will depend on the nature of the individuals and the areas of work.

DM: Do you think it may be easier to deliver this with full-time rather than part-time students who may perceive themselves to be on a specific occupational training route? Is there a conflict here between the short-term employer-led needs and the medium/longer term requirements of society and the economy in general?

MB: I think in some industries there is a conflict. If you look at those industries which have been used to a part-time mode of training, there is not much of a conflict, because I think over the period of years in which they have been running, employers have generally signed up to the breadth argument. But in other sectors, there is still a debate to be had.

One thing as well, while we are just talking about quality, which I think that the TEC needs to recognize, is the degree to which it requires providers themselves to meet certain quality standards. Now you will know that in the past we have had things like Approved Training Organization (ATO) certification, which I think served a purpose in that there was an objective measure of quality across a range of criteria relevant at a particular time. Nevertheless, because it was perceived as so objective, I have heard people argue it was not a 'true' measure of quality. It certainly wasn't outcome-based – by and large it was a measurement of processes, and I think we have to learn from that because I believe that the TEC does need a system something like ATO. The main options at the moment seem to be for the TECs to maintain something like ATO, using the 'Investors in People Scheme', or to introduce a procedure along the lines of 'Total Quality Management' (TQM) as another possibility, and we, among others, are exploring the value of BS 5750. But these processes all require a considerable investment of time. We need to be clear that such time is outweighed by the value of the outcome.

DM: A number of educational providers have looked at the British Standards, haven't they, although at the moment I do not know of one which has completed the process . . . do you?

MB: No . . . but there is at least one TEC that I know of which has committed itself to doing BS 5750 and will be requiring its providers to go through the same process. I think the TQM is a much more productive approach but at the same time is very resource-heavy, and probably needs the help of outside consultants to undertake customer perception studies, for example. There's much more than just a staff cost implication, there's a research consultancy cost as well.

DM: So you look like going for a TQM/ATO approach . . . ?

MB: Yes. That is our current thinking as far as TQM is concerned, we have begun to move along the road by trying to get an impression from employers of what they are expecting from the TEC. I think it is a process which will need to go on for a number of years, and I think it will have particular implications for management, it being the top-down process, which I think we have to take very, very seriously. I am sure as well that, having embarked on the process ourselves, we would require those organizations which we use to have similar processes, because I think it is important that across the whole of the TEC area there is consistency of understanding about what quality management actually is and the ways in which it is achieved.

DM: Do you see any problems in that different TECs may adopt different approaches to evaluating the concept of quality in themselves and their educational and training providers? There might be a danger in not having a national agreed standard of quality, don't you think?

MB: No, I don't see such a danger as long as all parties generally agree with the local standard and that it is based on factors which are important to the area. It has, however, to be said that there are some attractions to using something like a BS model because it is something which is internationally recognized. It is a clear demonstration of quality management, and it is something you can apply as an external standard to all the people you are dealing with. People know what the standard means. TQM is very much more variable because one might actually find that the TECs' customers in one area have different requirements from those in another, and that will inevitably lead to different approaches to quality management.

DM: In moving from BS 5750 to Total Quality Management as a means of maintaining and evaluating quality, I rather feel that we are moving from traditional models of training, in the production sense, to a more sophisticated approach more akin to higher and professional education. What role do you think the TEC might play as regards promoting higher and professional education in the future?

MB: Yes. It's still fairly early days yet and I suspect that our first plan is going to be fairly thin on higher and professional education. What is clear, however, from consultants' evidence is that we as an area, as you know Dave, are at some disadvantage because of our lack of higher education provision in general, despite the important contribution of your own institution [Suffolk College, Ipswich]. Certainly, all the economic indicators are that we shall need higher-level and professional skills much more in the future. Therefore, I think that the TEC's role will be one of trying to develop provision in those sectors first of all but on the back of clear employer pressure, because it is pointless creating a provision if employers don't then buy. It really has to be a partnership approach here. And I believe that we will argue for some interesting new approaches and in particular courses which do span industry and higher education, some of which I think will make more use of technological innovations and be based much more in the workplace using, perhaps, accredited tutors of the employer in partnership with college staff. So I can see special units or centres being developed, bringing together these skills and making them more accessible. I am very clear that the TEC will have to have a policy on higher education and it will be one which, as you know, is largely centred around the need for management development, recognizing that many managers need to be much more committed to developing themselves and people than they appear to be at the moment. I also think from that initiative a number of other interesting developments will emerge.

DM: That's very interesting and leads me into what I feel is an important area for consideration, which is the TEC's role in identifying education and training needs, given that quality provision is actually meeting the customers' requirements. How do you envisage that process continuing, as it is certainly critical to any long-term plan, isn't it?

MB: I think one of the things that will make our new organization different from the existing one is that, like yourselves, we will be forming a Research and Development Unit which will have to have a team of staff in it, not perhaps as large as we would like it to be, to look at different techniques of evaluation which we have already touched upon before in this discussion. The R & D Unit will have to look at quality development, taking on board new products as they progressively come on stream, including vocational qualifications. In this sense the R & D Unit will pick up the implications of new developments including, for example, total quality management. It will also have to pick up some sort of research function through employers which will constantly keep us abreast of what employers are needing from education and training.

DM: Presumably you see that R & D Unit as undertaking some of the impact evaluations referred to earlier?

MB: Yes. The Unit will have clear roles, one of which will be looking at the products currently being provided by education and training and the impact on the employer, trying to gauge future development and change. I also believe, that as a new organization, we have got to become very much closer to our customers at all levels, and I am strongly of the view that we must all have targets in mind about, for example, how much time we must spend with our customer. Time must clearly be allotted for that kind of customer care. I think that in turn takes us on to the debate about the way in which we will need to group ourselves to deal with our customers. At the moment, perhaps like yourselves, we tend to have an organizational model which has separate people dealing with Youth Training, and for Business Growth Training, and Employment Training, and so on. We need to develop through the TEC an organizational model which brings the responsibility for all our activities together, which focus primarily on the responsibility to our customers. Through this approach more information will be able to be fed into the R & D Unit to allow on-going evaluation to take place.

DM: Can I really push you now and ask you who you really think your customers are?

MB: It's going to be a fudged answer to some degree . . . it is easier to say our main customer is the employer because without the employer you don't get the jobs. But that ducks the issue, because you can have the best employers in the world, but if you don't have individuals committed to training and development and to employment, we shall continue to fail to match up to the performance of many of our overseas competitors. Therefore, we have to accept that we are clearly operating in a climate where our customers are employers and individuals, both of whom need to have a shared understanding about what they expect from the other. It is the same as the debate about education and training . . . it's all one when you come down to it. I expect from an educational institution, and I've heard many of your colleagues say, that your customers are individuals and you are about developing individuals. But those individuals do have employment expectations ultimately and you have to carry employers with you.

DM: Yes, it's back to the tradition of different professional groups, who pays and so forth . . .

MB: That's right.

DM: But what about the broader role of the funding bodies, the Local Authority, central government . . . there are some important notions of accountability there, aren't there?

MB: It's a weird one, isn't it? We talk about the government and Local Authorities providing funds and the person who pays the piper calls the tune. The fact is that the money which comes from those sources actually comes from people like us in the first instance: it comes from individuals, it comes from employers and consequently you still come back to the debate about those two parties being the clear customers. I think the role for government, however, is to encourage debate and thinking at a more strategic level than I think may sometimes be the case if you actually just left it to an organizational model which was about individuals and employers. The fact is there are economic priorities which the government can see much more clearly than people at local level and I think it is right for them to have an input to that. Equally, it is right for Local Education Authorities and the DES to have a view about the way in which education should be developed in the light of what they see nationally and internationally. And, I think it is right for them to see their views, perceptions, policies reflected in whatever plans providers decide to implement. But I see them in fact as only one of a range of customers and really I see them more as an influence. Mind you, I am sure if you ask politicians they might see it in a different way – you're asking a TEC Chief Executive this.

DM: I like your model of negotiation and partnership between the employer and the individual and I suspect that must be the way forward if we are to encourage the level of training and the level of development we actually need. I am very taken by your notion of evaluating quality based on working with employers and individuals once they have completed training. A number of organizations have R & D Units, our own College, the Local Authority – would you see some partnership developing there?

MB: Undoubtedly. One thing that has become clear from the TEC development phase in Suffolk, is the great deal of goodwill there is around different organizations to work collaboratively on some of this information, sharing data, sharing perceptions and reaching common understandings about future directions. I am not sure that's the same nationally and we must capitalize on this locally. There is nothing to gain by us all ploughing lone furrows as we have tended to do in the past – the sharing of resources has a lot going for it.

Broadening the point, I think that one of the things I have been very struck by in Suffolk, is the way in which the debate is beginning to take place around the importance of economic development, which as yet we have not touched on in this conversation. TECs were originally seen as about training and enterprise but my developing understanding is that the starting point really ought to be economic development. What sort of economy have we got at the moment, how is it felt that the economy should be developed and what contributions can training, education and enterprise make? You will know from the consultancy report, having been involved in it, that we have a county which has a disproportionately high share of industries which historically have shown little growth: the land based industries, the food industries, traditional engineering and so on. Arguably it is the 'high tech' industries we should be looking at more to develop a secure future. We must encourage a wider debate on such issues, and early indications are that enterprise- and economic-development people will work with bodies such as the TEC on a partnership basis, to develop a shared understanding of what needs to be done and how. That takes me on to another point, in that if you look at somewhere like Cambridgeshire or Thames Valley it is very clear that education and training actually helps to make important economic developments possible, and I think that we have a golden opportunity in Suffolk to develop along similar lines. Now in one sense none of that is about quality development, but it is about other influences the TEC ought to take account of and be encouraging a debate about, not necessarily as the lead organization, but perhaps in articulating an industrial and therefore employer view about the way in which things ought to be developing. I think from that will then come clear messages which at a strategic level we ought to be taking some account of in our education and training plans.

DM: What I find really quite fascinating and exciting is that you are actually moving, I think, to a much more what I would call second order level of quality . . .

MB: That's right . . .

DM: What I think you are saying, if I can just reflect your views so far, is that you are picking up the employer studies first, then moving on to issues affecting economic development. In doing this you are teasing out the notion of quality in terms of how successful the

TEC Board might be in facilitating economic development, and even beyond that, you are suggesting that these developments should lead to a new commercial and industrial investment in the Suffolk area. Therefore, your notion of quality is much broader . . .

MB: It is critical that education and training lead in the development of such initiatives because you are not going to get a new industry coming to the area unless they see a skilled base which they can capitalize upon. We must, therefore, think about a much longer-term strategic view within which we set aims, objectives and targets indicating where we should be in three, four or five years time. In Suffolk we are currently fortunate to be in an area of enormous economic development and growth, with little unemployment and where jobs are plentiful. Some may feel therefore, that we do not need to put in place medium- and longer-term plans for future economic development. I am not certain that this is the case, and we do have to look very carefully at the nature of our industry in Suffolk and the extent to which our education and training is matching the skill needs not only of the present but of the future. For example, we are becoming a major national and international centre for insurance and this must be an area in which we need to promote high quality education and training. Now, a collaborative model through which commercial and professional expertise is harnessed in line with educational and training needs, in partnership with such providers as yourselves, is a clear means of promoting quality education and training.

DM: Leading on from that notion of industrial and educational partnership, can I ask your views on the relationship between resourcing and quality?

MB: Yes . . . there is a relationship of course, there has to be. But I think resourcing is often only looked at in terms of financial input, whereas I think it is much wider than that, actually. I believe that without commitment and involvement of people the achievement of quality and the energy, creativity and hence innovation required is unlikely to happen. You don't achieve quality just by putting money in. Two issues therefore. One is that we must look at resourcing very widely and if you look at it on that broad scale there is a connection between resourcing and quality. The other point is that when it comes to financial inputs we have got to be much clearer about where we gain the most impact from the money we have around at the moment.

DM: This goes back to your notion of impact analysis again, doesn't it?

MB: Yes, and we could actually find that the multi-billion pound investment which is put into training nationally isn't necessarily always being spent in the most cost-effective way. This comes back to evaluation.

DM: Finally Mike, now that we have explored the whole concept of quality, including relatively straightforward performance indicators right through to a broader strategic analysis of quality in terms of economic development, if you were asked to sum up what is quality in vocational education and training, what would you now say?

MB: I think I'd need notice of that one! I can't do it in a simple fashion ... I think one thing that is pretty clear is that individuals and employers sometimes have a different perception of quality and I think we have to be working towards a situation where both parties have the same shared perception of what can be achieved. And, if you add to that as well the perception of the providers, those people that help in the achievement of quality, who may sometimes have different goals, then quality to my mind is when all these different partners agree and implement a shared understanding of what is right.

DM: Thank you. That to me is a very clear statement of the role TECs might play in facilitating the delivery of quality vocational education and training.

7 Delivering Medical Laboratory Sciences: A Case Study in Consultancy

Tony Barry

The South Glamorgan Institute of Higher Education was established on 1 September 1976. Based in Cardiff, it was formed by the amalgamation of the Colleges of Science and Technology, Food Technology, Education and Art. It is now one of the largest education establishments of its type in the UK and has an academic staff of over 450. These are supported by appropriate administrative and technical staff. Currently the student population exceeds 6000.

Since its inception, the Institute has achieved national and international recognition in providing a comprehensive range of educational and training facilities, tailored where necessary to meet specific requirements. The academic structure consists of five Faculties, these being Technology, Science, Education, Art and Design, Business and Liberal Studies. Students are recruited from both the UK and overseas. A number of modular inter-disciplinary and vocationally-orientated courses are also offered, thus providing a full range of professional qualifications.

Role of the Consultancy and Development Unit (CDU)

Following several months of discussion among senior staff, the CDU was established at this Institute in September 1986. The primary objectives of the Unit were to establish links with commerce and industry in the hope of attracting consultancy and training projects. These developments were envisaged as providing opportunities for staff and students to participate in and develop an ethos of 'enterprise'. Secondary objectives included:

- the sale and promotion of services, facilities and expertise available at the Institute;
- the establishment of mechanisms for increasing staff development;

- the provision of opportunities for raising the profile of the Institute as a major educational institution in the UK.

Experience gained during the first three years of operation indicates that the major thrust of the CDU's activities is now directed towards providing and designing specialized educational and training packages. Currently such programmes are in the areas of plastics, maritime studies, electronics, languages and environmental health. As industry, commerce and the professions become more aware of the value of re-education and retraining, increased demands for programmes in additional spheres are seen as inevitable.

Experience has also been gained in respect of survey work and feasibility studies, especially with regard to public bodies. Since these are seen as potential areas for future development, the Unit is planning a series of seminars tailored to meet the requirements of such a market.

Because of its innovative nature, the development of the Unit in its early days was largely reactive - much time and energy being devoted to identifying major strengths and assessing staff availability and motivation. The fostering of international links now forms an integral part of the College policy and as a consequence of this philosophy, major investments have been made in the Middle and Far East. Significant success has been achieved in the former region, largely as a result of active pursuit and identification of client bases. These included market research on potential student recruitment for mainstream activities and also the likely demand for specialist educational packages.

In September 1987 the Unit was provided with a unique opportunity to gain access to potential markets in the Far East when its Director was asked to participate in a Trade Mission (subsidized by the Department of Trade and Industry) to Hong Kong and China. This proved to be a very successful visit and as a consequence of this, he was asked to act as Director to a second Trade Mission, on this occasion to the Gulf States, Oman, Bahrain and Kuwait. Organized by the Cardiff Chamber of Commerce and Industry and consisting of 15 individuals, this 'high profile' mission took place in January–February 1987. This was at a time when the Gulf War between Iran and Iraq was coming to an end and confidence was beginning to return to the regional economy.

The organizational roles of the Director were many and varied. These included responsibility for arranging meetings at the respective British Embassies and participating in courtesy calls to Directors of Chambers of Commerce. The opportunity was also taken to increase the Institute's profile in the region and also to meet senior Government officials. It emerged from such meetings that opportunities existed in the Middle East for the development of specialized training courses in several areas,

areas, notably within the paramedical and environmental health professions. The remainder of this chapter is devoted to a case study centred on the development, provision and implementation of a training course for postgraduate paramedic personnel from the United Arab Emirates (UAE).

Background information

Health provision in each of the United Arab Emirates varies considerably. In Dubai, the Department of Health and Medical Services (DOHMS) is responsible for providing health care to a population of 338,500 inhabitants (1986). Table 7.1 provides information relating to medical services controlled by the DOHMS.

Facility/Patients	*Total Numbers*
Hospitals	3
Beds	1,624
Health Centres	14
Doctors	370
Nurses	1,630
Pharmacists	114
Technicians	515
In-Patients and Out-Patients	46,698

Table 7.1 *Health care statistics, Dubai.*

Health Services receive a high priority in the development plans of the Dubai Government. As part of a long-term strategy the authorities have sought to rationalize certain provisions within the Health Services. One of these includes the training of technicians working in Pathology Departments. The majority of these are involved in routine investigations within the general sphere of Medical Laboratory Sciences. Any attempts at providing adequate training programmes for this professional group are fraught with difficulties and these are compounded by a number of problems intrinsic to the UAE. These include the following:

- Organizational networks within 'Pathology' are unavoidably intricate. Seven or more specialist departments may be involved in each hospital. (This also applies in the UK.) Figure 7.1 illustrates the general infrastructure as applied to pathology services in Dubai.

- Not all senior technical staff (expatriates) perceive training of junior staff as part of their fixed-term contractual obligations.
- Since the establishment of the University of the Gulf at Al Ain, increasing numbers of female graduates have been produced. Although these have traditionally been restricted to employment within the Health and Education spheres, the Dubai government recognizes that this growing pool of well-educated young people represents a valuable core in terms of human resources. This is particularly relevant at a time when health care provision within the UK is expanding.
- The students currently graduating from the University at Al Ain have degrees in general sciences and do not necessarily possess an adequate knowledge and understanding of pathology and disease processes.

In an attempt at solving these difficulties, the College was asked to provide a specially designed postgraduate training programme for students of Medical Laboratory Sciences. This was to be based in the UK and of six months duration. The programme was to be aimed at providing

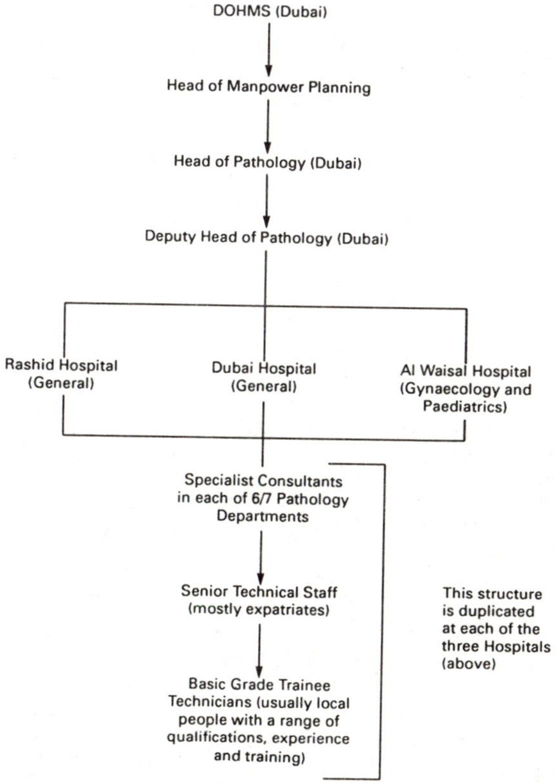

Figure 7.1 *Organization of pathology services, Dubai.*

opportunities to develop applied scientific skills required in the various disciplines of pathology and was to consist of integrated periods of college study and laboratory training.

Perceived initially as a pilot scheme, the programme was designed for a group of eight graduates. On their return to Dubai, these individuals would form the nucleus of a group of senior staff with responsibilities for staff development and training. An outline of the programme design is provided in Table 7.2. Part I of the course forms a common core of study for all students irrespective of specialist option. Part II represents study areas within each of the specialist areas. Part III was perceived as providing supportive Units.

Part I	Time (Hours)	Part II	Time (Hours)	Part III	Time (Hours)
Biology of Disease including:		*Specialist Option*		*Supportive Units*	
1. The Cell as a basis of life and disease.	9	Haematology and Blood Transfusion	120	Computers and Information	10
2. Cellular response to injury.	5	OR Medical Microbiology	120		
3. Aetiological classification of disease.	5	OR		Management Procedures	6
4. The Immune Response.	25	Clinical Chemistry	120		
5. Inflammation	10				
6. Pathogenicity	6				
7. Common pathological processes.	5				
TOTAL	65		120		16

Table 7.2 *College-based programme design*

Part IV of the course consists of fourteen weeks of hospital-based training. Students were to be placed in one of the specialized laboratories at the University Hospital of Wales in Cardiff under the direct supervision of highly experienced instructors. A continuous monitoring and assessment procedure was to form an integral part of a quality control process with regular reports made to the DOHMS. All students were placed in secure accommodation with a full-time housekeeper in attendance. Transport was to be provided as necessary.

The outline proposals were despatched to Dubai in the spring of 1988 and a 'follow-up' visit was made in May. As a result of this visit, the College was asked to make a number of minor modifications to the programme and the final draft was submitted and accepted in June 1988.

Course provision

The delegates arrived in the UK on 15 May 1989, were met by the Unit's Director at Gatwick and transported to Cardiff by luxury coach. Following an initial 'settling in' period of three days, the students commenced studies at the Institute. In retrospect it must be recognized that for any overseas student this initial period is an important one. Activities have to include the opening of bank accounts, registration with local police, finding a general practitioner, local tours, travel arrangements and introductions to people from their own country (in this case Arab nationals).

It soon became evident that the information provided by the DOHMS was incorrect in several respects. The students were not inexperienced as new graduates but proved to be highly intelligent, articulate and experienced scientists and already having a degree of seniority at their base laboratories. This fact alone necessitated a radical (and very prompt) rethink. Consequently, the first few days were spent in assessing requirements and developing a revised programme. Essentially this involved substantial increases in College-based units, particularly the Part I components. In addition, more tutorial and seminar periods were included since it was recognized that the students lacked some basic knowledge in pathology and disease processes.

Thereafter the College studies progressed well, the staff being impressed with the students' conscientious approach. Meanwhile the Director of the CDU had been appointed (unofficially) 'in loco parentis' for the female delegates. An important facet was the regular meetings which took place in order to overcome any problems that arose. One such problem that took some time to resolve was the installation of a telephone – an important link for visitors from an 'oil rich' State.

The hospital-based training element was re-organized to include eight weeks secondment to a modern district hospital and six weeks of short-term (2–3 days) visits to selected specialist laboratories in Cardiff. This was planned to provide the most appropriate 'blend' of training. In the event, transport proved difficult at first but eventually suitable arrangements were made. At least one of the specialist disciplines failed to provide the necessary range of training practices and this did prompt a number of complaints. Once again this necessitated some reorganization in an attempt to find suitable alternative accommodation.

At the end of the programme of study a joint meeting between students and staff was held to undertake a review of the course. The major recommendations made as a result of this meeting are outlined below:

- It was recognized that the balance between routine laboratory work (eg in a District General Hospital) and front-line technology (eg in a Teaching Hospital such as the University Hospital of Wales) should be determined by the experience and needs of students and achieved on an individual basis.
- Changes were proposed to the assessment format.
- That information should be made available in advance for prospective students concerning the type and range of equipment in use at the laboratories and information collected on the students' primary areas of interest in order to provide specialist option studies.
- A number of specific changes to the content were proposed including the provision of additional teaching support, offering more specialized modules to particular professional groups and, where possible, identifying subject areas of common interest to all students to bring the group together. It was also felt appropriate to include a programme of tutorials on wider issues in science, such as philosophical concepts in medicine.
- Changes in the structure of the course were proposed and it was felt by both staff and students that the existing sandwich modules should be replaced by part-time/day release arrangements. This, it was felt, could be made up of three days' laboratory training plus two days of College attendance per week throughout the course.
- It was recognized that significant differences exist between the UK and the UAE in terms of disease patterns. These would need taking into account when arranging visits to specialist laboratories in the Cardiff area and need identifying in advance.
- It was suggested that links be established with the appropriate national body which is the Institute of Medical Laboratory Sciences based in London, to offer the opportunity to exchange information and update students in current UK developments.

Conclusion

From the case study described, it can be seen that specialized training programmes of this type can pose problems in planning, organization and provision. Frequently, detailed information is lacking and often changes from original specifications are required. The rewards, however, can be most beneficial, to staff, students and the receiving country. The benefits and experience gained by this small but significant group of delegates from the UAE is difficult to quantify, but the friendships made and the relationships fostered will continue.

8 Go-Ahead Northern: A Case Study in Enterprise[1]

David Hind

Introduction

The purpose of this Chapter is to discuss how a successful educational partnership has been established with a major employer in Tyne and Wear – Go-Ahead Northern – and how this partnership has been used to produce a written case study for use with BA (Hons) Business Studies undergraduates.

Go-Ahead Northern is the UK's largest, privatized bus and coaching Company. Based in Bensham, Gateshead, Northern employs some 2200 personnel and operates a fleet of vehicles comprising 750 buses, coaches and taxis. Each year more than 140 million passengers are carried on Northern's network in the North-east of England.

The educational links with Northern have evolved over a three-year period. At the heart of the partnership is the written case study that has been produced in close collaboration with the Company. The case study is used with final year Business Studies undergraduates to develop further their business studies subject knowledge and their transferable personal skills. To add a commercial dimension to the exercise managers from Northern visit the Polytechnic to receive formal presentations from the students, and to question the students on their case study analysis and evaluation. Developing links with local employers and fostering mutually beneficial relationships takes time and effort from both sides.

Establishing initial contact

The Go-Ahead Northern Case Study evolved from a relationship with Northern that was quite well established. Northern in the mid-1980s was both a customer and a contributor to the Polytechnic. As a customer, Northern had used a range of consultancy and training services that are

1 Reprinted with permission from *Teaching and Learning Bulletin*.

provided for the local community. These services helped to establish the credibility of members of staff, and to create an awareness of the work of the Polytechnic in educating the young business managers of the future.

In addition to being a customer, Northern's managers also became contributors to the Polytechnic's activities. Senior managers from the Company were invited to the Polytechnic as guest lecturers, or as representatives of the local business community when special presentations were being made by students. These early links were instrumental in helping to build up a rapport and relationship between Go-Ahead Northern and the Polytechnic, but in particular a rapport between myself and Roger Rhodes at Northern (responsible for Business Development, Sales and Training). By identifying a manager who was interested in the educational world and who already had a favourable image of the Polytechnic it was possible to suggest that links between the two institutions be developed further by involving Northern directly with the BA (Hons) Business Studies degree.

The case study

One of the areas of concern in business education is that the availability of up-to-date case study material is in short supply. Another difficulty with case material is that the organization on which the case is based may be unfamiliar to the students. As a result of these concerns students sometimes find it difficult applying their intellectual skills to the problems that are set by the Course Team. One component of the Business Studies degree that relies heavily on the use of case studies is Business Policy.

In 1986 the UK bus industry experienced a major change in the way that the industry operated – deregulation. Deregulation opened up the bus routes in the UK to virtually free competition from any bus operator that wished to provide a stage carriage bus service. This major upheaval was followed by the privatization of the bus industry in 1987. Previously the regional and local bus companies were subsidiaries of the National Bus Company, but in 1987 these subsidiaries were to be sold to private buyers.

These two major changes to the bus industry were felt to offer considerable scope for analysis by Business Studies undergraduates within the Business Policy component. Thus, it was with this in mind that Roger Rhodes was approached at Northern, to see whether Northern would be willing to allow a case study to be written that documented Northern's response to deregulation and privatization. After agreeing the proposal with the directorate at Northern, background details of the Company and the industry were obtained through discussions with Roger Rhodes. The content of the case was supplemented by referring to published data produced on the national and local bus industry.

In writing the case study, however, it has to be stated that much attention was paid to ensuring that no confidential material was included in the case, only material that was of a general publishable nature. Northern carefully edited the case to ensure that no commercially sensitive data or information was being reproduced. The wishes of Northern were carefully followed at all times in order to preserve the goodwill that had previously been established.

Implementing the case study

The purpose of the case study is to enable the students to apply their business knowledge and transferable personal skills to a Company that is familiar to them. As with all case studies only a certain amount of information can be communicated through a written document. Thus, in addition to the case study it was decided that further background information would assist the students with their analysis of the case. To do this two approaches are adopted. Firstly, to supplement the factual information in the case, Roger Rhodes visits the Polytechnic and makes a formal presentation, providing the students with information on the current activities of Northern. The students also have the opportunity to question Roger on points they wish to be elaborated. Second, to give the students an idea of the resources available to Northern, and what the Company is like 'behind the depot doors' visits have been organized to two of Northern's bus depots. Here, a tour is provided of the depot, and the students are given another brief presentation by a Company manager, this time looking at the operational side of the business.

Now that the students have a clear picture of Northern and the bus industry, the next stage in the case study analysis is for the students to apply their intellectual skills to solving a business-related problem. The exact nature of the problem changes each year. The first time that the case was used the students were asked to suggest business strategies that could be implemented by Northern to take advantage of opportunities posed by deregulation and privatization. The most recent problem put to the students has required them to look at Northern's approach to providing a 'quality' bus service, and to recommend ways that the quality approach can be enhanced further.

When the problem has been analysed and recommendations produced, the next stage in the case study is for the students to present their findings. This is normally done in two ways. First, by each individual student writing a formal report that details their analysis of the case. Second, by means of formal oral presentation, on a group basis. In December 1988, the most recent time that the case was used, the formal oral presentations were made to five managers from Northern. Each manager was joined by a member of the Course Team and received 15-minute presentations from the students. The purpose of the presentations was to persuade the manager to implement a new procedure that would lead to an improved quality of service being provided for members of the travelling public. Once the formal presentation had been made, the students were then questioned by the manager, on their proposals.

The final component of the case study is that of providing feedback to the students on their analysis of the case study, and their success at persuading the manager to implement a new procedure. Northern are again involved in this process which is felt to be an important part of the exercise.

Typically, the Northern Case Study is implemented over a four-week period, occupying a three-hour, half-day slot each week:

- Week 1 – Formal presentation by Northern;
- Week 2 – Visit by students to Northern depots;
- Week 3 – Presentations by students to Northern's managers;
- Week 4 – Feedback to students on their analysis of the case and their transferable personal skills.

It is clear from the above that much co-ordination and liaison takes place between the Polytechnic and Northern. Typically there are 55 students studying Business Policy, and planning the logistics of the exercise is extremely time consuming. However, it is felt that the benefits of running the case study far outweigh the costs, benefits that accrue to Northern, the students, and to the Course Team.

The benefits of the case study

All the parties involved with the case study gain from being involved with it. From Northern's perspective, they feel that one of the benefits that is derived is that of having regular contact with lecturers from the Polytechnic. When meeting to discuss the case study the opportunity can be taken to explore how modern business theories might be applied by Northern. Northern's management is kept up to date with current developments in marketing for example, and a contact is available to them at the Polytechnic whereby informal discussions can be held on marketing-related topics.

When the students analyse the case study and present their findings Northern receives the objective business views of 55 bright young people. While the students will not have an in-depth knowledge of Northern, they might be able to bring their experiences as business students and consumers of the bus services to bear on their case study analysis.

Northern can also take the opportunity to appraise the students as potential graduate trainees of the future. Students who might be particularly interested in a career in the bus industry can be identified through the operation of the case study. Indeed, the students' awareness of Go-Ahead Northern is enhanced and when a student project is to be completed it might be that a student decides to undertake a project on behalf of Northern.

The students also gain from the case study. Feedback questionnaires that have been completed by students indicate that they do appreciate being able to pit their intellectual skills against a major local Company that they are familiar with. The visits to company depots add another dimension, enabling them to get a feel for the culture of the Company, and the attitudes of the employees. By making presentations to managers from Northern a touch of realism is injected into the case, and the actual process of making a presentation to someone they have not met before is challenging.

From a transferable personal skills perspective a wide spectrum of skills have to be mastered to complete the exercise successfully. Group-work skills are called into use. Verbal and non-verbal communication skills are tested. The high-order intellectual skills of analysis, synthesis and evaluation have to be applied to the exercise. In addition to these skills the students are to some extent working as consultants for Northern, and have to gather information in order to draw conclusions.

The Course Team also benefits from the exercise. By discussing the case with Northern the opportunity is taken to see how closely academic theories are applied in practice. The link that has been fostered has allowed the author to undertake an industrial secondment with Northern that has proved to be mutually beneficial.

Thus, although much effort has been involved in developing the case study considerable benefits do accrue to all concerned. Having discussed the details of the Go-Ahead Northern Case Study it is now pertinent to draw together some of the lessons that have been learnt about its development.

The lessons learnt

Considered below are some of the lessons that have been learnt from developing the case:

- Developing a case study in this way requires the injection of considerable time and effort by all concerned. Time needs to be made available to establish links with the industry in the first place, and then to nurture such links for mutual benefit.

- To gain credibility with the host organization a 'professional' approach has been adopted by the Polytechnic, and members of staff, at all times.
- The wishes of the host organiztion have to be accepted wherever possible. If certain information is felt to be too confidential for dissemination to students, then this information should be withheld.
- Contact needs to be maintained with the host organization throughout the academic year, not only when the case study, for example, is being implemented.
- Every effort should be made to reward the host organization for the contributions they do make to the education of our students. Clearly, it is difficult to offer financial incentives, but the opportunity can be taken to encourage students to undertake projects on behalf of the host organization, or for staff to undertake industrial secondments.
- The host organization needs to feel that its contributions are welcomed by the Polytechnic as a whole and not simply by the Course Team in question. Involving the Directorate of the Polytechnic in any exercises that are organized can help in this way. Indeed, in December 1988, when the Go-Ahead Northern Case Study was last run, the Deputy Director of the Polytechnic was involved and offered hospitality to Northern's managers. This gesture was greatly appreciated by the students, the Course Team, and Northern's managers.

Conclusion

The purpose of this Chapter has been to provide an example of how a successful educational partnership has been established with a major local employer. The Go-Ahead Northern case study has evolved and developed as a result of the determination and perseverance of the members of staff concerned from both the Polytechnic and Northern. While considerable time and effort is needed for developing links with local employers in the first place, and maintaining the links once established, the benefits that accrue from the exercise are such that they outweigh these costs.

PART IV

Quality: Product Control and Institutional Perspectives

The main focus in Part IV is on ways in which educational institutions have introduced procedures of quality assurance. Explicit in the total quality approach is ensuring that the product being delivered is defect free. In terms of education and training this requires that evaluation is built in on a continuous basis. Specifically, this implies that programmes of study be systematically monitored and evaluated and special emphasis be placed on the quality of the students' learning experience. However, in building in quality to course provision there are always broader institutional considerations. Part IV explores product control as part of the course review process and managerial perspectives within a changing external framework of vocational education.

The case study by Norris (Chapter 9) describes in detail the introduction of an effective course-monitoring and -evaluation process. This contribution is particularly interesting in that it offers guidelines on how to introduce a course review process into an institution which hitherto had not given product control priority. A clear policy commitment at senior managerial level within the College was formally adopted by the Institution's Academic Board, which led to the process of implementation at the level of Faculties and Schools. This resulted in a detailed and sophisticated process of product control. This points heavily to the value of there being an institutional commitment to product control, for there to develop involvement and participation from tutors directly involved in teaching.

Chapter 10, by Guri, outlines a process for ensuring the quality of distance-learning materials. It complements the case study by Norris in that it details a number of procedures to be followed. The development of open learning materials is of major importance, given the developments taking place in vocational education. It is likely that there will be a significant increase in open and flexible learning to encourage employers to take advantages of the training opportunities at a relatively low cost in staff time. There is a consequent need to ensure that the material produced is of a sufficiently high standard to make it easy for students to gain the necessary knowledge and skills.

However, although both the approaches included in Part IV are necessary components of a quality assurance process, they are not in themselves sufficient to ensure that the organization is delivering quality. The two Case Studies illustrate putting in place procedures which identify the service targets and objectives, which might be referred to as 'quality standards', and processes which ensure that the standards are met, that is 'quality control'. Of greater importance during the next decade will be the introduction of broader approaches to the delivery of vocational education and training which seek to build quality in rather than control poor practice out. This is the notion of quality assurance discussed earlier in Chapters 1 and 2. This approach has as its aim to ensure defect-free products and, at a broader institutional level, to make quality the focus of the teaching and learning process.

Applying the principles of 'Total Quality Management' to programmes of educational study is paralleled by similar concerns at institutional level, in wishing to go further than the use of relatively simple output measures to evaluate quality. There is, of course, a considerable debate on the use of performance indicators in public sector service industries, especially health and education. Performance indicators are defined by Cave et al (1988) as measures usually in quantitative forms, of institutional attributes, relating to the activity they undertake. In relationship to higher education, Cave et al define eight performance indicators relating to teaching:

> entry qualifications; Degree results; cost per student or staff/student ratio; value added; rate of return; wastage and completion rates; employment on graduation; student and peer review (p 106).

It can be seen that most of these measures relate either to input or output and not directly to the teaching and learning process. The inclusion of student and peer reviews focuses on teaching, which again is an input variable, whereas 'value added' and 'rate of return' relate input variables to outputs. These performance indicators are relatively 'cold' measures of the effectiveness of vocational education and cannot be interpreted in terms of the total quality movement, which would argue that there is insufficient focus on building quality into the process.

This is not to decry the use of performance indicators which are now becoming significant means within further and higher education of being seen to be publicly accountable. There remains, however, the danger identified by Allsop and Findlay (1989) that performance indicators focus on what can easily be measured rather than on what should be evaluated. A survey of the development and use of the performance indicators in universities across fifteen countries showed that they were used primarily for the allocation of human or financial resources (Cuenin, 1987). There are serious reservations about the use of performance indicators if they are not built into a broader institutional perspective on quality assurance. Furthermore, it is of major concern that in the large number of performance indicators available there is minimum reference to students' learning and to strategies which focus on making it easy for the learner.

The contributions by Stanton, and Aitken et al, in Chapters 11 and 12, are directly concerned with the institutional implications of the introduction of National Vocational Qualifications (NVQs). In both these chapters it is clear that this initiative has placed significant emphasis on the outputs of learning and on students acquiring competences matched to the workplace needs. The specific curriculum implications for such an approach are highlighted by Aitken et al who argue for the need to develop a modular flexible approach which enables students as customers to gain vocational qualifications. Stanton goes one step further in arguing that the introduction of NVQs places a much greater requirement for lecturers and tutors to act diagnostically in terms of assessing students and for the focus of learning to be clearly with the prospective student. The ownership of the learning process in such an approach transfers to the customer, and tutors can be seen as facilitating this process by offering educational counselling. At the level of further education, the introduction of NVQs is beginning to have a significant impact, both from the perspective of employers and students themselves. Moreover, it can be argued that this change is beneficial to the learner in that he or she does not need to proceed through traditional programmes of study to obtain vocational qualification.

Yorke, in Chapter 13, develops the same theme in relationship to higher education. He argues that it is necessary to go beyond the course review procedures which have been developed hand-in-hand with CNAA in promoting public sector education, towards the introduction of institutional audits. Implicit in this theme is an expectation that institutions will enable students to be placed at the centre of the learning process. This implies that the organization itself will have a 'corporate statement of purpose' or a 'mission statement', so that its client group is aware of its aims and objectives. A working paper produced by CNAA (1989) concludes that developing institutional self-appraisal will:

- provide each institution with a composite profile of its own educational performance;
- do justice to the institution's self-chosen goals, while reflecting the key common features shared by institutions of higher education;
- encourage institutions to develop their own individuality (p 11).

The Further Education Unit (1989) has produced more detailed guidelines on encouraging institutions to carry out an educational audit. This project identifies a number of topic areas for consideration at an institutional level, all of which reflect quality. These include the purpose of the institution, its management procedures, the use of resources and final outcomes. These approaches encourage a broader perspective on vocational education and training than might be gained by students within a framework which focuses specifically on their programmes of study. This is not to deny the importance of the teaching process but to recognize that institutions offering vocational education and training need to be customer-driven and to provide a service which enables students to negotiate their own learning. The transfer of responsibility to the learner goes beyond the design of courses and is the responsibility of those managing and leading institutions offering education and training.

References

Allsop, P and Findlay, P (1989) Performance indicators and course quality developments in the public sector. In M McVicar (Ed) *Performance Indicators and Quality Control in Higher Education*. Portsmouth: Portsmouth Polytechnic

Cave, M; Hanney, S; Kogan, M and Trevett, G (1988) *The Use of Performance Indicators in Higher Education*. London: Jessica Kingsley

CNAA (1989) *Towards an Educational Audit*. London: CNAA

Cuenin, S (1987) The use of performance indicators in universities: an international survey. *International Journal of Institutional Management in Higher Education* 11, 117–39

FEU (1989) *Towards an Educational Audit*. London: FEU

9 The Theory and Practice of Course Evaluation: An Analysis of the System introduced at Suffolk College

Keith Norris

This chapter is concerned with the use of course evaluation in assessing the effectiveness of educational institutions. Unlike most commercial companies financial performance, and in particular profitability, can not be used as the fundamental measure of performance. Alternative strategies have, therefore, to be devised. The use of course evaluation is based on the assumption that the development of the abilities and intellectual capacity of students through the provision of educational programmes is the main function of educational institutions. The quality and effectiveness of course provision is, therefore, regarded as the most important variable in assessing institutional effectiveness.

Evaluation at course level is concerned with input measures in terms of resource utilization, process measures with respect to teaching and learning strategies and output measures as indicated by student success and their perception of the quality of the teaching and learning strategies employed. Students are regarded as the clients of the organization and courses in all their forms as the product range. The course team is therefore of fundamental importance in determining the quality and effectiveness of the product through critical course appraisal and the implementation of appropriate course developments.

Background

Suffolk College is a large mixed economy college. It has a wide range of course provision including school-linked 'A' Levels, traditional and 'new' non-advanced further education, and advanced further education, as well as being responsible for a substantial programme of adult and community education. The college employs over 300 full-time equivalent academic staff and has approximately 30,000 students of which 14,000 are engaged on qualification courses resulting in 4,500 full-time equivalent students of which 800 are engaged on advanced programmes.

Two major organizational developments have taken place during the past two years, which have been of fundamental importance to the development of the process of course evaluation:

- management restructuring; and
- the introduction of a policy statement on the management of courses emphasizing the role of course committees and course leaders.

Both developments emphasize the importance of course committees and although not specifically addressing the issue of course evaluation provide the foundation necessary for developing an effective system of course evaluation.

Management restructuring

Prior to reorganization in 1987 the management of the college was based on a traditional departmental structure. Although course leaders and course teams were identified, it was common practice to have a number of sector heads within departments who were responsible to the Head of Department for both resource management and academic provision.

Managerial emphasis, including academic developments, was predominantly based on the seniority of staff rather than through course leaders and course committees. Course teams in the main were concerned with course administration and maintaining the 'standards of the course'. The latter involved setting assignments and examinations of the 'right' level and ensuring students were graded accordingly. Heads of Departments were responsible for reporting examination results to the appropriate faculty board.

Following widespread consultation, Academic Board and Governors accepted proposals to introduce a two-tier structure based on faculties and schools. In addition three cross-college units were introduced. Course management below Head of School is now vested in course committees, each with a defined course leader. Although some principal lecturers have responsibilities for course development, course committees, through the course leader, are directly responsible to the Head of School for the quality and development of their respective courses. The importance of course committees is therefore emphasized within the new structure. Faculties have been defined as strategic managerial and policy-forming units with a critical role in relation to academic and educational processes, especially course developments and the process of course evaluation.

Policy statement on 'The Management of Courses'

Subsequent to the implementation of the new management structure consideration was given to the formation of a college policy statement with respect to course management. Securing the support of both senior management and academic staff was considered to be of the utmost importance to the successful implementation of a unified system of course evaluation. This was achieved by the production of a number of discussion papers which were circulated widely. This resulted in a policy paper which was adopted by the Academic Board, defining the membership of course committees, together with their terms of reference and the responsibilities of the Course Leader. The terms of reference include:

- the maintenance of academic standards;
- the formal monitoring and evaluation of the course and reporting to the Faculty Board or other parts of the academic structure;
- establishing an effective means of student/staff liaison, to obtain the views of past and present students on the course;
- receiving reports from External Examiners and taking appropriate action.

In addition to academic staff, students and, where appropriate, representatives from external clients groups are members of the course committee. Although the process is not defined, course committees are clearly responsible for carrying out an appropriate level of course evaluation and presenting a report to the appropriate Faculty Board and on to the College Standards Committee which is a Sub-Committee of the Academic Board.

The course evaluation system and its development

Before reorganization in November 1987 the only college-wide procedure for evaluating the effectiveness of course provision was the annual reporting of examination results. In a number of cases this requirement had been extended to include a report from the Head of Department highlighting aspects requiring explanation of discussion. The report together with a tabulated presentation of all the examination results was presented to the appropriate Faculty Board and subsequently to the Academic Board. The degree of course monitoring, except for the reporting of examination results, varied across the college. Due to the absence of any procedures to which every course was subjected, a pragmatic approach had been adopted over the years and more often than not in response to the requirements of particular validating bodies. Consideration of teaching and learning strategies appropriate to specific groups of students and the development of action plans attracted very little or no attention.

Factors influencing development

The move towards a more formal system of course evaluation was made in response to the increased importance attached to the quality of provision, the need for management information and the requirements of a number of external agents. The model shown in Figure 9.1 highlights the more important factors. A discussion paper presented to the Academic Board in March 1988 identified the following factors in proposing that the college should move towards a formal system of course evaluation.

- The recognition that the most important function of the college relates to the learning and teaching process and this needs to be under constant review in the light of the quality of student experience and the academic health of the course being provided. It was emphasized

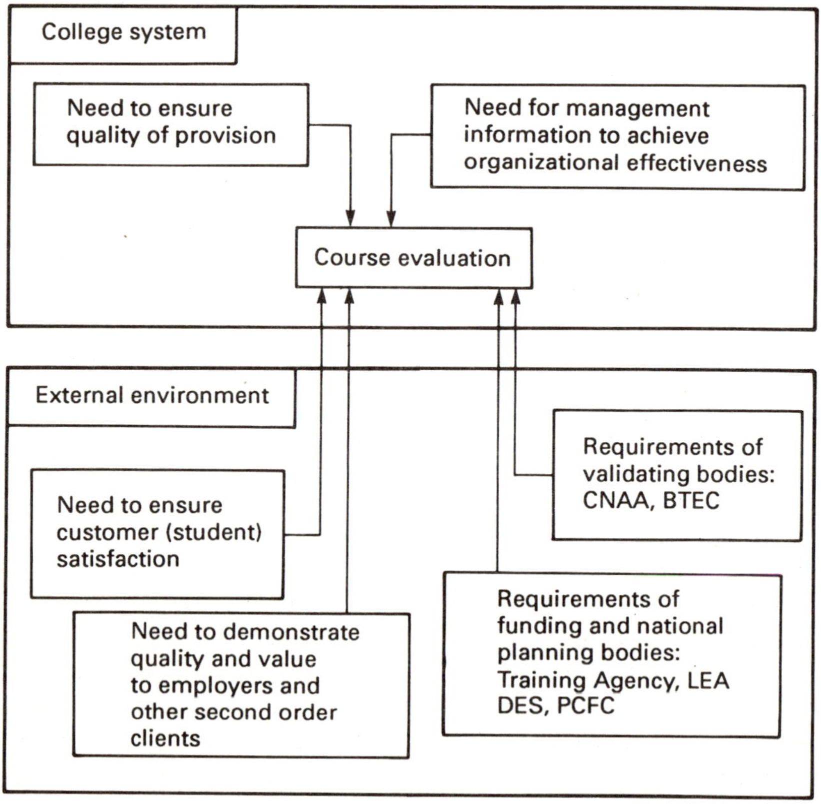

Figure 9.1 *Factors influencing the development of a formal course evaluation system*

that this process should be qualitative and that all monitoring data should be subject to careful consideration and interpretation.

- The need for a central co-ordinated approach from which to develop institutional policies and to provide an input to a centralized management information system in influencing the strategies adopted for the allocation of resources.
- The requirement of external agencies, including validation and accreditation bodies, highlighted the need to develop more sophisticated and co-ordinated institutional procedures.

These factors illustrate the dual requirement of course evaluation processes. The first is concerned with improving the quality of course provision. Course committees are responsible for carrying out the review process which is intended to facilitate course developments and teaching and learning strategies. Second, the process should provide information on the cost and effectiveness of course provision. Although related to quality this is intended to provide information to support managerial decision-making. In fulfilling the requirements of the institution the process should be capable of satisfying the demands of external validating bodies and other external agents (see CNAA 1988; BTEC 1988; MSC 1985).

The system

Although the Academic Board agreed the principles governing the development of a course evaluation process, at its meeting in March 1988, faculties were left to develop a system and procedures that satisfied their own specified requirements. The emergent system will, however, be evaluated with a view to establishing a significant level of conformity across the college. In response the Faculty Board for Technology addressed the issue and agreed to discontinue the 'old' process of reporting examination results together with summary reports from Heads of School in favour of a system of individual course evaluation reports. The system adopted required course committees to carry out a review and evaluation for all courses run during the academic year and to submit a summary report to the Faculty Board via the appropriate Head of School. There were five main elements involved in the process: course data; student perceptions; moderator reports; peer review; and recommendations for change.

Although the process was relatively successful many course teams experienced significant difficulty in carrying out a self-critical review of the course and in preparing a meaningful report. Following the completion of the first round of course evaluations a working party of the Faculty Board reviewed the process and recommended the following changes.

- An impartial sub-committee consisting of the Head of Faculty and one representative from each of the constituent Schools was formed to monitor course evaluation reports. The sub-committee was to provide a summary report to the Faculty Board.
- A course evaluation check list was developed in order to facilitate critical discussions by course committees.
- The course data sheet was amended to make it easier to complete and to provide information on a complete cohort of students.

It was also accepted that the process of course evaluation, and in particular the requirement to be self-critical, was new to most members of course committees and presented a number of problems. The importance of providing a programme of staff development aimed at achieving a common understanding of the benefits to be derived from systematic course evaluation as well as developing the skills and confidence required to be self-critical cannot be overstated.

Due to the continuing difficulty being experienced by course committees in producing course evaluation reports the Faculty Sub-committee is in the process of developing a set of detailed guidelines. Although still in the early stages a list of the important aspects have been developed and accepted by the Faculty Board (see Table 9.1). The proposals are in part based on the system developed at Sunderland Polytechnic (Webster and Biott, 1979).

Although the main purpose of course evaluation is to improve the quality of course provision it is important that the information produced is capable of supporting the managerial decision-making process. This is illustrated in the systems diagram presented in Figure 9.2. An account of the use of systems diagrams to illustrate and analyse managerial processes can be found in the work of Checkland (1981).

Evaluation of the system

The system presented was developed in the belief that it should focus on the educational experiences offered to and received by students (CNAA, 1989). Consequently one of the main aims of the process is to facilitate improvements in the quality of the student experience. The measures used therefore provide course committees with the information necessary to review the quality and appropriateness of the course, identify key issues and take the necessary action. Within the institution, however, performance indicators constitute an essential element in the management decision-making process; the information obtained is used to formulate strategic policies and to make judgements on the allocation of resources. A third aspect concerns the requirements imposed by external bodies.

Initially these were almost exclusively concerned with cost and efficiency. More recently, however, funding bodies have begun to accept the importance of quality. This is evidence in the increasing use of output-related indicators as opposed to a total reliance on input measures. The report of a study on efficiency in non-advanced further education recommended that 'all colleges build into their management procedures the collection and use of output indicators identified in the report. These should help to ensure that inputs are not emphasized at the expense of outputs, and that efficiency and effectiveness are considered together' (DES, 1987).

The distinction between the three aspects of course evaluation is identified by Cave in considering the use of performance indicators by funding bodies external to the institution, as a basis of resource allocation across institutions and as a means of educating and guiding members of the institution (Cave et al, 1988). The distinction between the various uses of performance indicators is also stressed by Cuenin (1987) who identifies two main areas of use internal to the institution and communications with external bodies.

Wider views of the multiple constituency approaches are presented by Kanter and Brinkerhaff (1981) and Batten and Trafford (1985) both of which identify a wide range of stake-holders. The system described attempts to satisfy the requirements of four main sub-groups (see Figure 9.3), which are very closely related to the findings presented above.

The student as the consumer of courses is involved in the process by the use of student feedback questionnaires and by representation on the course committee. The information derived from this source is essential to facilitate course developments. The course data sheet provides a range of input and output measures to provide the information necessary to make managerial decisions and satisfy the requirements of external bodies as well as supplement the student feedback process.

The multi-dimensional aspects of evaluation are presented and developed in a different context by Thomas (1987) who considers the structures and relationships that exist between the various interested parties engaged in educational evaluation. The parameters used by Thomas explore the relationship between 'Autonomy' or 'Control' processes and Internal or External evaluations. This is closely related to the distinctions drawn by Cave in which external bodies would be regarded as exerting control and the internal process exhibiting differing degrees of autonomy. The concept of autonomy or control can also be applied to the institutional setting in exploring the relationship between the course committee and management as well as the use to which the information derived is put. Thomas develops this further by differentiating alternative models of conduct, as shown in Figure 9.4.

1	*Course Information Feedback*	
1.1	Course data	Identification of issues raised by the information provided on the course data sheet. Note: the course data sheet to be submitted as part of the report. Where applicable retention rates, success rates, destinations, etc, should be referred to.
1.2	Employer feedback	Analysis of feedback for employers on the course committee and other relevant sources, eg training groups, employers' federations, student placements, employer questionnaires.
1.3	Student feedback	Feedback from students including analysis of student questionnaires, interviews, consultative sessions, representatives on course committees, etc.
1.4	External examiners	Summary of the main issues identified. Specific problems and achievements should be highlighted.
2	*Course Delivery and Management*	
2.1	Course delivery	Course content, teaching and learning methods, assessment schemes. Developments should be evaluated and proposals for future changes identified in the action plan (section 3).
2.2	Course mangement	Staffing, accommodation, developmental requirements, etc. Where possible the course committee should identify priorities.
2.3	Course marketing	Strategies for marketing and student recruitment.
2.4	Staff development	Outline of staff development undertaken during the academic year and identification of future requirements/priorities.
3	*Evaluation and Action Plan*	
3.1	Evaluative summary	The appraisal by the course committee of all the above sections. This part of the report must therefore be valid in terms of the information contained on the course data sheet, feedback from employers and students and the professional judgement of the course committee.
3.2	Action plan	Details of actions to be taken during the academic year together with an indication of longer-term developments.

Table 9.1 *Framework for the production of course reports*

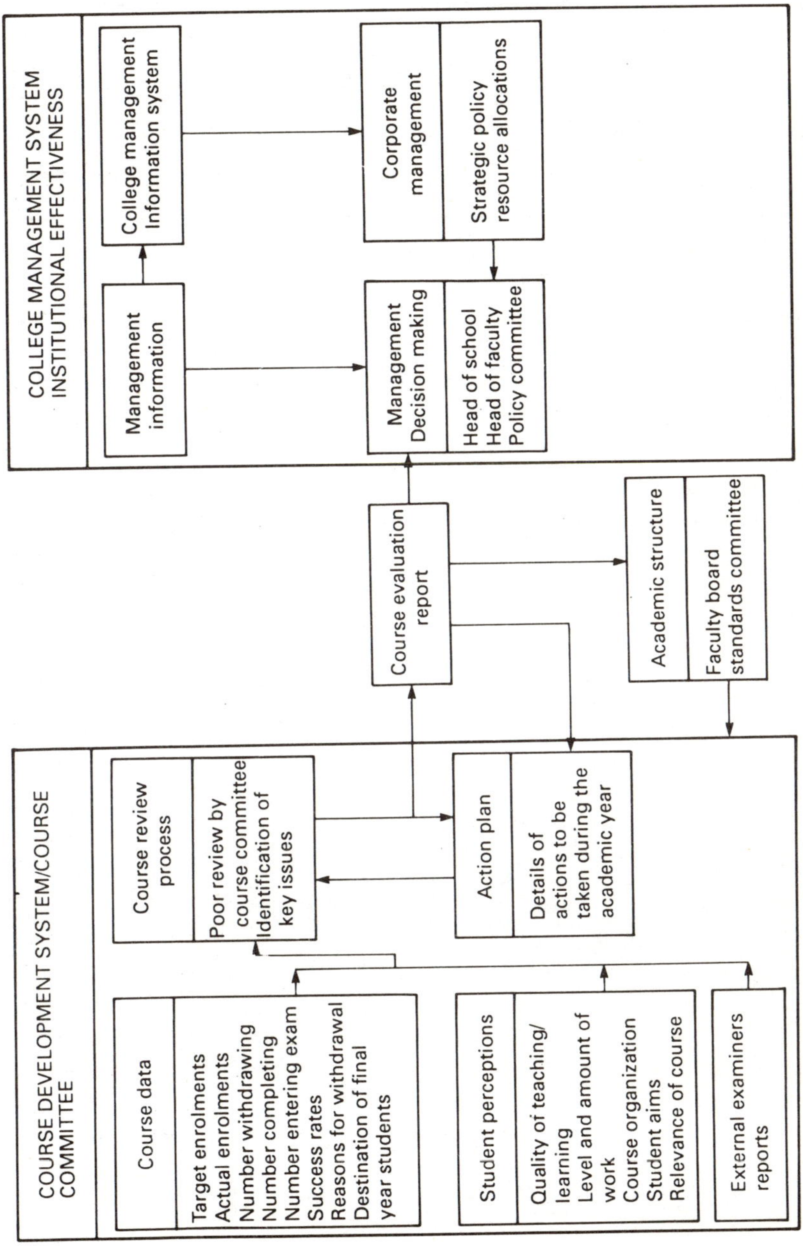

Figure 9.2 *Contribution of course evaluation to course developments and managerial decision-making*

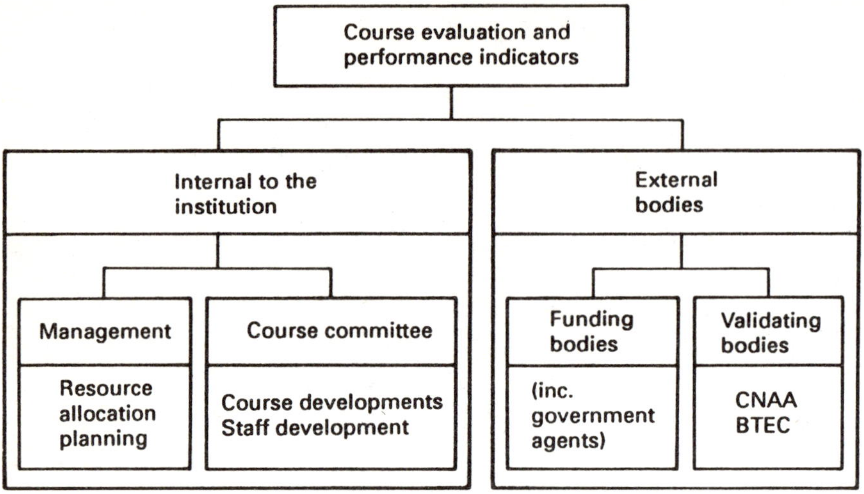

Figure 9.3 *Principal users of the evaluation process*

In many respects the model would suggest incompatibility between the requirements of the various interested parties. Course development is best achieved by having open judgements and negotiated criteria; managerial decision-making dictates the use of 'standard' indicators while funding bodies attempt to impose criteria. As a consequence the system used is in many ways a compromise between the desire to focus attention on facilitating course developments via course committees and the need to provide predetermined indicators for use by the management decision-making process, and to satisfy external bodies. The system developed

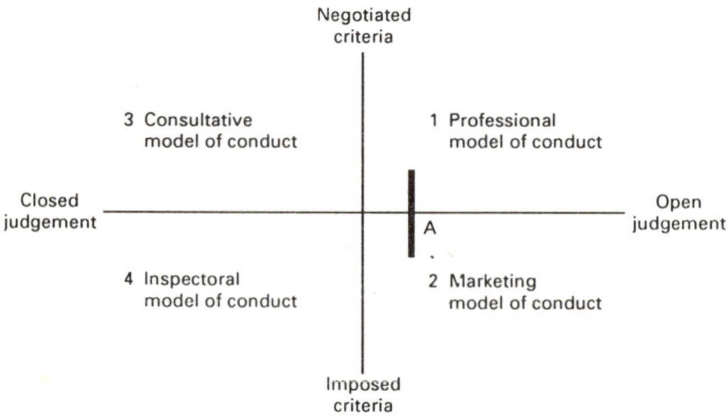

The area covered by the system adopted is signified at ▌A

Figure 9.4 *Conduct within evaluation relationships* (Source: Thomas, 1987)

therefore exhibits aspects of both the Professional and Marketing Model of Conduct as illustrated in Figure 9.4.

All judgemental processes within the college are conducted as openly as possible. The process of evaluation is participatory, with course committees considering the various indicators, forming judgements and developing action plans. The course report and action plan is presented to the appropriate Faculty Board and ultimately to the Standards Committee which is charged with ensuring that an acceptable level of evaluation is conducted throughout the institution. Although course evaluation reports are produced each year the system represents a continuous process, with the outcomes of one year's review feeding the next. In considering this aspect Elliott (1979, p 6) suggests that measures of accountability for teachers that do not engage them in a participatory process seem doomed to fail at the level of implementation.

Use of performance indicators

A variety of interesting methodologies for classifying performance indicators have been suggested (Carlisle, 1972; Cuenin, 1987; and Cave et al, 1988). The two most important dimensions presented are concerned with the stage in the process measured by the indicator and the type or category of indicator used. The indicators used in the system presented in this chapter are classified accordingly in Table 9.2. A further distinction is also drawn between subjective and objective data.

The range of indicators developed, including those derived from student feedback, moderators and peer review, is regarded as adequate to facilitate course committees assessing the quality of provision and instigating the necessary developments. Although satisfying the current requirements of external bodies the measures of efficiency are largely based on input measures. The need to develop more sophisticated measures based on output has been identified as being necessary in the near future (DES, 1987). These will include: cost per enrolled student, cost per student completing the course, the cost per qualified student (Birch, 1988).

Validity of the system

Following a review of a diverse range of models developed to assess organizational effectiveness, Cameron (1980; Cameron and Whetten, 1983) identified a seven-construct decision guide for classifying systems of measuring organizational effectiveness. The results of applying the model to the course evaluation system discussed here is presented in Table 9.3. For the purpose of the analysis each aspect of the seven critical questions is rated according to the degree to which the system addresses

Type of category / *Stage in the process*		*Input*	*Process*	*Output*
Cuenin	*Carlisle*			
Simple	Descriptive	Enrolments ■ Qualifications ■	Number withdrawing ■ Reasons for withdrawing ■	Destination of students ■
Performance	Normative Evaluative Predictive	SSR's ■ ASH ■	Wastage rates ■ Student perceptions of learning methods, course managements ■	Pass rates ■ Employment rates ■ Staying on rates ■ Completion rates ■
		Examiners/Moderators ■ Peer Evaluations ■		
General	Informative	Market survey ■/■ Employment trends ■/■	Course committee structure ■ Frequency of meetings ■	Requirements of Higher education ■

Table 9.2 *Classification of performance indicators*

Critical question		Degree to which the system addresses the question: High	Medium	Low
1 On what domain of activity is the judgement focused?	(a) Academic	■		
	(b) External adoption			■
	(c) Extra curricular		■	
	(d) Morale		■	
2 Whose perspective or which constituency's point of view is considered?	**Internal**			
	(a) Individual member of staff		■	
	(b) Course committee	■		
	(c) School management		■	
	(d) College management		■	
	External			
	(a) Funding bodies		■	
	(b) Validating bodies	■		
	(c) Government agencies		■	
3 What is the purpose for judging effectiveness?	(a) Individual staff development		■	
	(b) Improved quality of course provision	■		
	(c) Efficient use of resources		■	
	(d) Effective use of resources		■	
	(e) Satisfy external bodies		■	
4 What level of analysis is being used?	(a) Individual member		■	
	(b) Course group	■		
	(c) School group			■
	(d) Faculty group			■
	(e) Overall Institution			■
5 What time frame is being employed?	(a) Short term (less than one year)			■
	(b) Medium term (one year)	■		
	(c) Long term (up to 5 years)		■	

Table 9.3 *Multi-dimensional analysis of the course evaluation process*
(continues over)

Critical question		Degree to which the system addresses the question: High	Medium	Low
6 What type of data are being used	(a) Objective data			
	input	■		
	process		■	
	output		■	
	(b) Perceptual data			
	Student perception	■		
	Peer review	■		
	External moderation	■		
7 What referent is being employed?	(a) Comparative		■	
	(b) Normative			■
	(c) Goals		■	
	(d) Improvement	■		
	(e) Organizational characteristics		■	

Table 9.3 *continued*

and the compatibility of the elements assessed.

Although the system was designed to satisfy a range of requirements, the analysis indicates a high level of consistency in the areas scored high in terms of the degree to which the system addresses the various aspects. As indicated in the earlier sections, the use of course evaluation as a measure of institutional effectiveness is based on the assumption that the provision of educational programmes is the main function of the institution.

The evaluation process therefore focuses on the quality of course provision (questions 1 and 3). The course committee is regarded as the level at which the important behaviour occurs and the predominant referent is that of improving the quality of provision (questions 4 and 7). Although a range of indicators capable of satisfying the requirements of multi-constituencies are used, the dominant perspectives are those of the course committee and validating bodies (question 2). The data collected also emphasizes student perceptions, peer review and reports from external moderators (question 6).

In itself the system is, however, weak in its ability to measure the institution's success in adapting to changes in demands from customers and providing aggregated data with respect to the effectiveness at School, Faculty or Institutional level. Care must therefore be taken to ensure that the unit cost information provided by the management information system is capable of satisfying the requirements of the last-named. The Institution's ability to adapt to changing need will have to be assessed outside the course evaluation system.

Conclusions

The evaluation system presented here represents a move away from the use of rigid output measures in the form of examination results towards a process of quality assurance. The system developed is primarily concerned with improving the quality of course provision and consequently enhancing the students' experience rather than with managerial control. The focus of the process must therefore reside with the course committee who have direct responsibility for course design and development. In order to maintain the professional model of conduct the system should be open both in terms of the criteria used and the judgements made. It is also important to ensure that all aspects, including the level of analysis, the time frame employed, the type of data used and the referent employed, are compatible with the philosophy adopted. This is illustrated in Table 9.3.

Although much of the course data and the production of the course review report is formalized in an annual cycle, course review should be regarded as a continual process. Issues should be identified as they occur, considered in relation to the overall aims of the course, appropriate action taken and the outcomes reviewed. In this respect it is important that the outcomes of one year's review are considered as input to the next. This ensures that the effectiveness of action plans are continuously reviewed and developed.

A second, but important, aspect of course evaluation is concerned with the provision of the information necessary to facilitate managerial decisions with respect to the effective use of resources. The output of the process is an essential element of the management information system. Equally, where possible the management information system should be used to reduce the work of course committees by providing basic course data. Course evaluation therefore simultaneously makes use of and contributes to the management information system.

Third, it is important that the requirements of external bodies who have a legitimate interest in the effectiveness of course provision are satisfied. In this respect a number of standard performance indicators may have to be incorporated into the process. It must be accepted therefore that although the main focus of course evaluation is concerned with facilitating course developments a compromise has to be achieved with respect to the effective use of resources and the need to satisfy the requirements of external bodies.

The introduction of a formal process of course evaluation should be regarded as only the first step. The most important and in many ways the most difficult phase is concerned with ensuring that course teams develop the competence and confidence to be open and self-critical. Practices and attitudes learned in response to the previous culture will have to be disregarded and new ones learnt. Staff development programmes have to include activities that develop the competence and confidence to be self-critical. In this respect it is essential to ensure that management resists the temptation to intervene in situations where course evaluation reports identify marginal performance. Course teams should be encouraged to implement their own actions and control procedures.

The implementation of a 'developmental' system of course evaluation should be regarded as a continuous process that requires time and encouragement to evolve. As with all change strategies, its success is dependent on four key elements:

- the commitment of senior management;
- the validity of the processes introduced;
- the involvement of staff at all levels;
- the provision of an adequate programme of staff development.

References

Batton, C and Trafford, V (1985) Evaluation: an aid to institutional management. In G Lockwood and J Davis (Eds) *Universities: The Management of Change*. Windsor: NFER-Nelson and Society for Research into Higher Education

Birch, D (1988) *Managing Resources in Further Education: A Handbook for College Managers*. Bristol: FESC

BTEC (1988) *Course Review and Evaluation: General Guidelines*. London: BTEC

Cameron, K S (1980) Critical questions in assessing organizational effectiveness *Organizational Dynamics* 9, 66–80

Cameron, K S and Whetten, D A (1983) *Organizational Effectiveness: A Comparison of Multiple Models*. London: Academic Press

Carlisle, E (1972) The conceptual structure of social indicators. In A Shonfield and S Shaw (Eds) *Social Indicators and Social Policy*. London: Heinemann

Cave, M; Hanney, S; Kogan, M; and Trevett, G (1988) *The Use of Performance Indicators in Higher Education*. London: Jessica Kingsley

Checkland, P (1981) *Systems Thinking: Systems Practice*. Chichester: Wiley

CNAA (1988) *Handbook*. London: CNAA

CNAA (1989) Quality assurance systems and issues for consideration. *Development Services Briefing*, 16 May, London: CNAA

Cuenin, S (1987) The use of performance indicators in universities: an international survey. *International Journal of Institutional Management in Higher Education*, 11, 117–39

DES (1987) *Managing Colleges Efficiently*. London: HMSO

Elliott, J (1979) Accountability, progressive education and school-based evaluation. *Education*, 3-13, 7, 27–31

Kanter, R M and Brinkerhaff, D (1981) Organizational performance: recent developments in measurement. *American Review of Sociology*, 7, 321–49

MSC (Manpower Services Commission) (1985) *Work Related NAFE. A Guidance Handbook*. London: MSC

Thomas, H (1987) Perspectives on evaluation. In M Hughes, P Ribbins and H Thomas (Eds) *Managing Education: The System and the Distribution*. London: Cassell Educational

Webster, H and Biott, C (1979) Course Evaluation at Sunderland Polytechnic. In D Billing (Ed) *Indicators of Performance*. Surrey: Society for Research into Higher Education

10 Quality Control in Distance Learning[1]

Sarah Guri

Quality refers to a product's fitness for purpose according to a set of required standards. *Quality control* is primarily an action which adjusts operations to predetermined criteria. Although some consider this approach to be inapplicable to education, many components of control procedures are implicit in managing educational processes (Marsh, 1983; Wheeler, 1983). Quality control mechanisms are used by policy-makers and practitioners in education to ensure particular standards of quality in relation to intended goals, the scope and structure of curricula, learning-teaching processes and student achievements. In higher education the management of quality commonly takes place in areas such as faculty recruitment, general policy decisions and student assessment, but rarely extends to the evaluation of the quality of teaching or study materials.

Quality control mechanisms in relation to academic teaching create considerable conceptual and practical difficulties. The concepts of academic freedom and professional autonomy assume that what goes on in a particular educational institution, course or classroom is the responsibility of the professional concerned. This rests on a view of the individual 'as professionally competent over a full range of activities he undertakes, and this competence includes the necessary knowledge and skills to make or seek insightful and valid appraisals of his work and to act on those appraisals' (Adelman and Alexander, 1982, pp 15–16). The professional retains control over the key evaluation decisions of *what* to evaluate, *how* to evaluate, *to whom* to disseminate findings and *what* actions to take in the light of them.

Despite the pervasiveness of this view in higher education, criticism has been growing in recent years. Astin (1980) has argued that most measures of institutional quality in higher education are inadequate in today's policy environment. In Astin's view, the pedagogical skills of college faculties are one of the most under-developed resources in higher

1 Reprinted with permission from *Open Learning*, 1987, 2, pp 16–21.

education and 'concentrating more of our energies on the development of these skills could prove to be the most productive and self protective activities that institutions can engage in during the next 10 years' (p 19). Believing that higher education institutions must become far more student-orientated than at present, Astin defines a high-quality institution as 'one that knows what's happening to its students and one that gives faculty clear-cut opportunities to develop their teaching skills'.

Similarly, the quality and feasibility of course proposals or curriculum packages in higher education are rarely subject to a thorough evaluation. In many cases, the appraisal process is no more than 'a rubber stamping formality at faculty or Senate level which ensures that the outward forms of a proposal - title, syllabus and examination arrangements - are consistent with the prevailing practices' (Adelman and Alexander, 1982 p 9).

In contrast to the conventional universities, many of the distance-teaching universities encourage team working, and use control procedures for the evaluation of self-study materials. The design and development of distance-learning courses at Everyman's University, Israel, are subject to several stages of quality control, from the very early phase of defining the theme of a course to its final stage of editorial and graphic layout. These mechanisms will be analysed in the light of their substantial and potential contribution to the improvement of academic teaching. Before doing so, Everyman's University and its learning system will be briefly described.

The learning system of Everyman's University

Everyman's University (EU) was established in 1974 by the government of Israel and the Rothschild Foundation. It was inspired mainly by the remarkable achievements of the Open University in Britain. In the summer of 1980, the Israel Council for Higher Education recognized EU as an institution for Higher Learning and authorized it to award a Bachelor's Degree. Today EU is firmly established on the educational scene with 12,000 students and over 200 courses. Eighteen courses are required for a degree. Each course has a printed text (usually 700–1,000 pages divided into 12 weekly units, each unit requiring 15 to 18 hours of study), which is supplemented by relevant learning aids. Prestigious universities in Israel and elsewhere readily accept its graduates for postgraduate study.

EU is what its name declares it to be; a university open to everyone. It has no admission requirements, and its students are drawn from the widest spectrum of backgrounds and age groups, and are widely dispersed geographically. The fact that the students learning at EU and their study

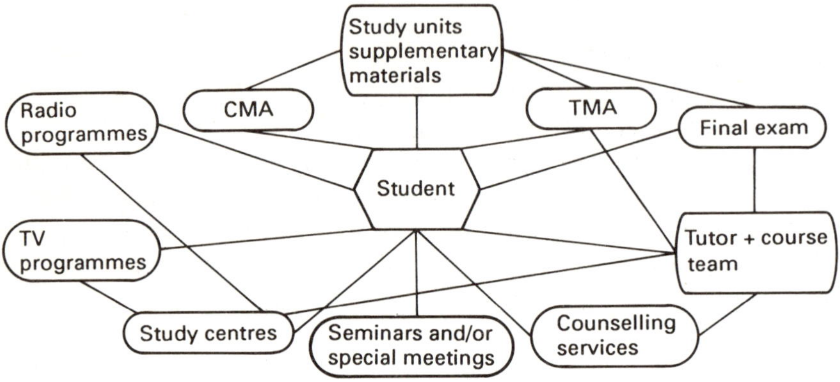

Figure 10.1 *Components of the learning system in Everyman's University*

conditions differ significantly from the traditional university required the design of a totally new learning system. It was possible to do this without having to tackle the problems of implementing innovations into an existing system (see Figure 10.1).

Course approval procedures

The need to employ special control mechanisms for course approval in EU was influenced mainly by its model of operation. From the very outset, EU intended to base its academic work upon a nucleus of internal faculty members working together with outside contributors from other major Israeli universities. Its planners determined that it was impractical for the new institution ever to build the kinds of specialized faculties which characterize traditional universities. In 1985–6, EU had a full-time senior academic staff of 22 lecturers and professors, and 15 faculty from conventional universities who were spending their sabbaticals or leaves of absence there. Six professors were also employed without academic appointments, bringing the faculty total to 43. Several hundred scholars from other universities are utilized on short-term contracts to consult, to write and to re-write varying portions of courses. The co-operative work between internal and external faculty and the continuous recruitment of outside contributors led to the creation of special course approval procedures, described in Figure 10.2.

The recruitment of external authors is done in several ways which range from personal acquaintance to a systematic search for experts. Guidance is crucial for outside contributors, since they are not aware of the special characteristics of EU's learning system. Jenkins (1983 pp 319–20) specified several models for training writers in distance-teaching universities; training by correspondence, self-tuition, intensive workshops, and in-service training involving an editor and a writer working closely together. EU uses an alternative model in which the outside contributors are personally guided by the internal academic staff. The matching between the guide and the author depends on the specific subject-matter. Obviously, in courses using both internal and external authors, these authors need to work as a team from the very first stage of the proposal design. All authors receive guidance on the elements that compose distance-learning materials, and are advised how to write course proposals and prepare sample materials.

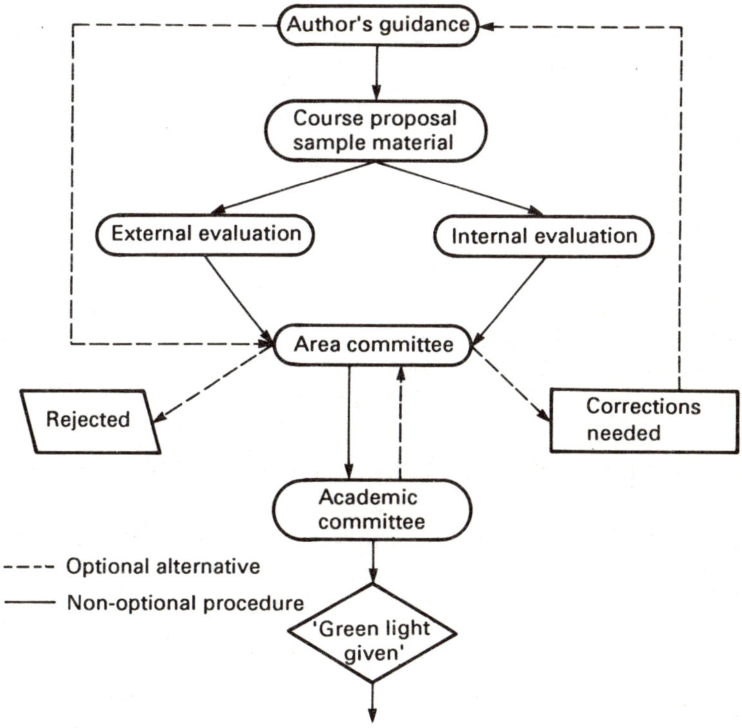

Figure 10.2 *Course approval procedures*

The decision to request sample materials from authors resulted from a series of previous failures, in which written units did not meet the structure and format requirements of instructional self-study units. Even brilliant scholars with an outstanding reputation in the academic world can fail to transfer their knowledge and expertise into an instructional written discourse. Writing distance-learning texts requires skills which are often quite different from those associated with lecturing in a conventional university. Some external authors are shocked and surprised when they are presented with challenges to their assumptions about teaching and are forced to rethink how they should present their subject. Many resist training or criticism.

Moreover, part-time external staff lack the institutional commitment of full-time permanent staff. Conflicting loyalties among part-time writers may result in the production of material which is unsuitable for distance learners. Also, because of the academic freedom they have previously experienced, they may be reluctant to allow any modifications to be made to their work by the permanent staff (Carr, 1984 p 17). Naturally, the contracted authors are much more concerned with the students in their own institution than with the special needs of distance learners. Many of them may be too busy to devote sufficient time and energy to the development of self-study courses.

In the course proposal the author (or authors), whether from outside or inside EU, is asked to specify the following:

- the theme of the course;
- its function in the subject programme (eg how does a course on 'curriculum design and development' fit into the educational master's programme?);
- its level (introductory, regular or advanced);
- the prerequisite of the course;
- its overall goals;
- specific learning objectives;
- the structure of the course and its division into learning units;
- audio visual equipment to accompany the units;
- prospective radio and/or television programmes to be developed;
- the academic staff who will comprise the course team;
- proposed academic consultants to whom the study units will be sent for evaluation.

The course proposal is usually sent to three or four experts in the field, working at other Israeli universities or abroad. Some of the evaluators may be internal faculty. The sample material is mostly commented on by internal staff who are acquainted with EU's materials and standards. Course proposal evaluators are asked to comment on the following:

- the scope and content of the course as reflected in the specified goals;
- the structure of the course and its division into sub-themes;
- the appropriateness of the content to the course's specified level.

The advice of the outside experts is intended to illuminate each proposal from a variety of possible perspectives, and to enable EU's internal subject committees to discuss and criticize them constructively. The evaluation of the sample study units by internal staff relates to the clarity and pedagogical quality of the written materials.

Subject (area) committees then discuss each proposed course in the presence of the author(s). In such meetings three alternative decisions might be reached:

- to approve the development of the course;
- to approve it with restrictions in case there are revisions needed;
- to reject it.

Around 30 proposals are discussed in the various subject committees each year. Approximately 20 per cent are rejected on the grounds of inadequacy or poor-quality materials, and another 20 per cent require re-drafting. Decisions are taken by a majority vote of the subject committee's members. If corrections are requested the author is advised how to go about them. Sometimes the subject committee will reassemble to discuss a revised proposal. Minor corrections, on the other hand, are sent to the committee's members individually for comments. If the course is approved without restrictions the subject committee submits its decision to the Academic Committee, EU's higher academic authority.

The Academic Committee is made up of EU's academic faculty members and professors from other Israeli universities, and is chaired by EU's president. Only rarely does the Academic Committee reject the subject committee's decisions. Nevertheless, its members might ask for clarification and require changes or reconsideration of various elements. The fact that the Academic Committee is comprised of people from a broad spectrum of disciplines and universities enables it to perceive the development of a specific course in the context of the total system. This is especially beneficial when dealing with an inter-disciplinary course. If the Academic Committee approves a proposed course, a 'green light' is given and it enters the developmental phase.

Course design and development

Course development generally requires 18–48 months, the greatest proportion of that time being devoted to the writing and re-writing of the text by the course team. Figure 10.3 describes the design and development process of EU's study materials.

The *comprehensive course team* includes all the academics involved in writing the study units and a course co-ordinator, whose task is to regulate the work of the team and to provide a link between the authors and the others participating in the course production process – editor, graphic designer, media library, typing service, publishing office, etc. Course co-ordinators have either a Master's degree or are doctoral students in the specific course area.

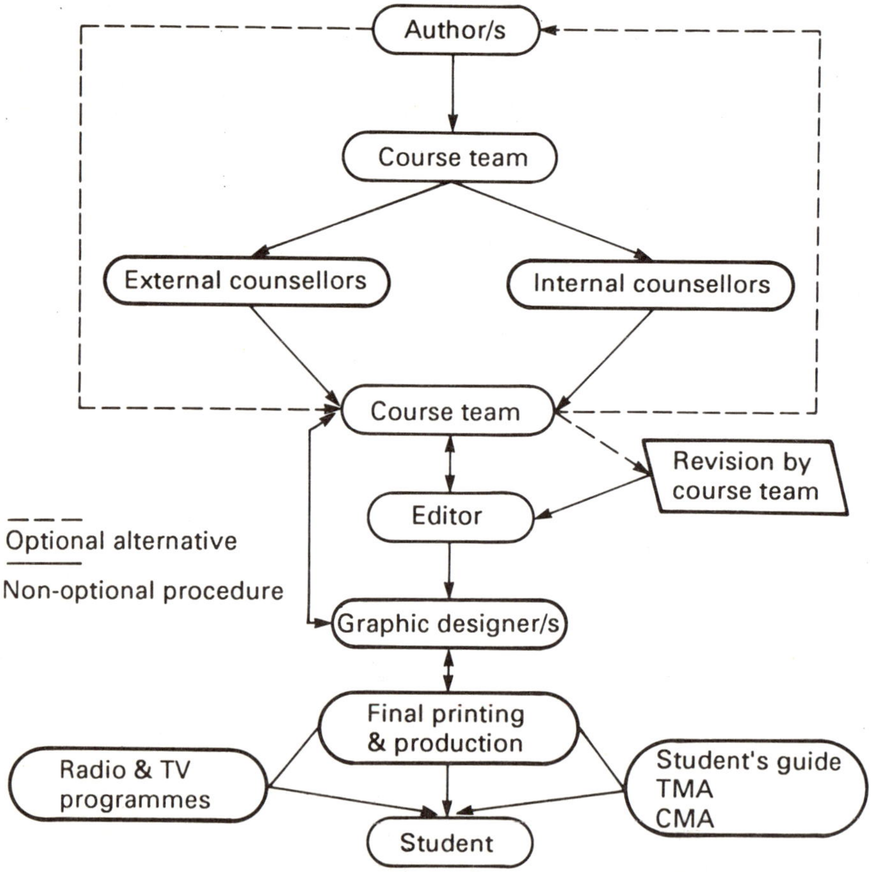

Figure 10.3 *Course design and development*

A course may be written by several authors or just one, but there is always a course team chair who is responsible for the scope and content of the total course. The course team chair determines the course curriculum and methodology and directs the other authors, and, together with the course co-ordinator, constitutes the *nuclear course team.*

Successful co-operation between the nuclear and comprehensive course teams depends mainly on two factors: the participation of an internal academic as a course team chair, and the management skills of the course co-ordinator. Courses which are chaired by an internal academic face fewer co-ordination problems and tend to be developed in a shorter time when compared to courses written totally by external authors. In the latter case, the skills of the course co-ordinator, who may also play an important role in rewriting the learning materials, are crucial. Between 15 per cent and 20 per cent of approved courses are dropped in mid-production due to problems, but over 200 courses have now been successfully completed.

Whether the writer is an external expert or an internal faculty member, the first draft of each study unit is addressed to the nuclear course team. If they do not recommend any drastic or significant changes, it is sent to two to four external and/or internal experts in the appropriate field for their comments and suggestions.

Evaluation of study units is carried out on the basis of the following questions (the order does not imply any priority):

- Is the material up to date and accurate?
- Are the explanations clear and fluent, and do they meet the standards of self-study materials?
- Are the presentations interesting and stimulating?
- Do the learning activities incorporated into the presentations enhance learning and assist the student in understanding the main points and critical issues?
- The study unit is designed for 15–20 learning hours. Does the scope of the material meet this criterion? Is it overloaded, or is it too limited?

The aim at this stage is to analyse the content and instructional quality of the learning materials carefully and critically. By using the intellectual resources of other universities, EU hopes to upgrade academic instruction through collective criticism and intensive brain-storming.

If most of the evaluations recommend a revision, the nuclear course team meets with the author. Some authors take it upon themselves to revise or even rewrite the study unit, while others pass the mandate to the course team, mainly the course co-ordinator. Occasionally, a unit has to be rewritten by a different author. In all cases, the nuclear course team has an important role in deciding on the instructional design of each unit.

The uniqueness of EU's quality control model

EU's quality control mechanisms may be analysed by comparison with other models described by Smith (1980). Smith classified course development procedures in distance teaching universities into five broad categories:

- the course team model;
- the author/editor model;
- the contract author/faculty model;
- the educational adviser model;
- the intuition model.

EU's model combines some essential components of the 'course team model' and 'the contract author/faculty model', adding to them its own unique elements.

The concept of the course team, consisting of academics, television and radio personnel, editors and graphic designers was developed by the British Open University. But the Open University has a relatively large full-time internal academic staff who write most of the units for its undergraduate courses, whereas EU operates with a very small number of full-time faculty. This fact influences significantly the nature of the quality-control mechanisms aiming at producing a high-quality end-product in each of the institutions. Most of the formative evaluation procedures in the Open University are carried out by the internal staff, who are committed to the institution, available for regular discussions and acquainted with the teaching standards. In EU great energy is invested in guiding external scholars, and in ensuring a flowing communication among the team members. Obviously, in teams consisting largely of outside contributors, 'communication among them and the co-ordination and integration of their individual contribution in terms of content, pedagogy, etc, are more difficult to achieve' (Carr, 1984 p 18).

In such circumstances, the role of the internal faculty (including the course assistant) becomes critical in initiating, co-ordinating and revising the external writers' work. On the other hand, the scarcity of internal experts leads to a greater reliance on outside scholars for the evaluation of each unit's content and scope.

The contract author/faculty model is used by universities relying on external contributors. According to this model outside experts are contracted to write a course (or a unit), 'but the material is vetted by the full-time faculty of the University' (Smith, 1980 p 65). Smith stresses that 'this [model] enables courses to be developed much more quickly than would happen under a course team arrangement, but significant amendments and revisions to the original drafts are much more difficult to effect under this system'.

The basic elements of the contract author/faculty model exist in EU, but with substantial modifications. First, the drafts of external authors are subject to the same quality control procedures as those written by internal faculty. Quite often the external work requires much more revision than the materials written by internal staff. Hence the development of courses based heavily on outside experts usually takes more time than those produced by full-time faculty teams. Second, the contracted authors in EU are part of a course team while engaged in writing their study units. Their materials are not merely evaluated by the internal staff. They are involved in the process of decision-making during all the stages of course design and development.

EU's model allows a flexible policy of course planning, since it is possible to employ a wide range of specialists on a part-time basis, without being restricted to the particular interests of the tenured staff. Most especially, EU offers substantial potential for improving instruction in the traditional universities. EU has contributed to the Israeli higher education 'by paying pre-eminent attention to effective pedagogy and by addressing the crucial question, "What is quality in higher education?". As hundreds of professors from around the country have come to be involved in EU's work, the spin-offs for improved teaching elsewhere cannot be doubted' (Halperin, 1984 p 99).

Nevertheless, one should be aware of overlooking certain pitfalls which lurk behind the quality control of academic work. Many scholars feel reluctant to go through such stringent procedures and refuse to co-operate with EU's faculty, and most of the work prepared by external academics requires intensive rewriting. A partial solution to the problem might be the recruitment of full-time temporary staff on longer contracts. It might increase their loyalty and commitment to the institution while engaged in writing a course, and decrease their initial resistance to being criticized and evaluated by peers. Another solution might be the extension of the nuclear full-time faculty at EU, so that at least one internal academic could participate in each course team.

EU's model provides an illuminating example of how a small staff can manage efficiently a relatively large-scale distance-teaching operation, by tapping the intellectual resources of other universities and using special quality-control procedures. It might be of special interest to distance-teaching universities in the Third World, as well as for well-established universities, such as the Open University, in resolving the problems of large course teams.

References

Adelman, C and Alexander, R (1982) *The Self-Evaluating Institution.* London: Methuen

Astin, A W (1980) When does a college deserve to be called 'High Quality'? *Current Issues in Higher Education*, 1. Washington: American Association for Higher Education

Carr, R (1984) Author employment in distance teaching universities. *ICDE Bulletin*, 6, 16–20

Halperin, S (1984) *Any Home a Campus: Everyman's University of Israel*. Washington: The Institute for Educational Leadership

Jenkins, J (1983) Tell me how to write. In D Stewart, D Keegan and B Holmberg (Eds) *Distance Education: International Perspectives*. London: Croom Helm

Marsh, D (1983) The production model of quality control and its application to human resources in education. In O Boyd-Barrett, J Bush, J Goodey, I McNay and M Preedy (Eds) *Approaches to Post-School Management*. London: Harper & Row

Smith, K C (1980) Course development and procedures. *Distance Education*, 1, 61–7

Wheeler, G (1983) The implications and processes of quality control in further and higher education. In O Boyd-Barrett, J Bush, J Goodey, I McNay and M Preedy (Eds) *Approaches to Post-School Management*. London: Harper & Row

11 The Contribution of Further Education Colleges to Delivering NVQs[1]

Geoff Stanton

Introduction

In discussing this issue, I shall not be referring to any particular examples of National Vocational Qualifications. A major problem for Further Education Colleges in coming to terms with the implications for them of competence-led NVQs is the great variability in the pace and extent of change in different vocational sectors. In some sectors, significant changes have already occurred. In others, change is still some way off. Most tricky of all, some sectors have seen change, but the new qualifications have only received conditional accreditation. That means that further developments will occur, with the colleges being uncertain of their timing and extent. Nevertheless, it is possible – and, I believe, useful – to analyse the impact of the NVQ approach and philosophy in 'ideal' terms.

It is possible through creating a stereotype of a new qualification, and noting that its design-base is so radically different from what has gone before that it will not just be a matter of retraining those staff who provide work in the vocational education and training systems. The systems themselves will need to be redesigned. It is useful to explore this stereotypical situation, in order to identify the nature of the final destination to which we are heading. The extent of the institutional changes which colleges will need to undergo is such that they need to be planned on a whole-college basis over a significant period of time. Managers therefore need a model to work on in planning their strategy.

This is in any case necessary if the changes are to be conducted efficiently and effectively, while protecting the interests of current clients.

1 Reprinted with permission from *Competence & Assessment* 1989, 9, pp 11–13.

But it is even more necessary at a time when many other developments are impacting upon the colleges. These include the introduction of Training and Enterprise Councils, reformed governing bodies with new powers, and an increase in the average age of the learners in FE colleges because of demographic trends.

While most colleges are at least considering the implications of all this, few have yet had time to analyse what the advent of the National Curriculum in schools will mean for them. It is not just that school-leavers will arrive with new and different skills and understanding. They and their parents will have become used to new ways of having their progress and attainment measured and reported.

One set of implications is related to the fact that FE colleges also offer school-type courses (or link with schools in order to make pre-vocational provisions available). Not only are over 40 per cent of A-level students in FE, but many school-leavers and adults make use of FE to improve their GCSEs. Another set of implications is concerned with the interface between school qualifications performance and NVQs. These are explored below.

I believe that it is (fortunately) the case that as long as the institutional changes are in the right direction, and significant enough, the same restructuring and reorientation can enable all the above to be effectively handled. The purpose of giving this introduction is both to amplify the need for change, and to encourage FE's partners in the system to offer sympathetic support.

The support is not just needed for the sake of the FE colleges. Without the effective operation of the FE system – consisting as it does of more than 400 LEA maintained colleges employing the equivalent of 63,000 full-time lecturers – neither the ambitions of NCVQ nor of the Industry Lead Bodies can be properly achieved.

The place of teaching

Some would say that the fundamental change is away from qualifications based on the acquisition of either knowledge or skill (or a combination of both) and towards competence-based qualifications. Certainly, the challenge of enabling learners to meet standards of competence as defined by the industry will be a considerable one, not least because I am sure we shall find that we do not always understand as much as we hoped about how competence may be developed.

However, FE staff have had the assessment goal-posts moved before – from topics to objectives, or from end-tests to continuous assessment, for instance. If it were just that what is being assessed is to be changed then we would be able to wheel out old change mechanisms in order to cope.

Nor is the proposal to facilitate credit accumulation and transfer that earth shattering. The old Technician Education Council, and even the Open University, operated Unit-based assessment. No, the really radical change can be described as follows: Many learners used to gain a qualification by passing a course. In future, it will NOT be necessary to take a course at all to become qualified.

In other words, if an individual can demonstrate that his or her performance matches the definition of competence as laid down by the Industry Lead Body (ILB), that person may be awarded the relevant qualifications simply on that basis. (Remember, this is a simplistic model. In the real world, the means of accumulating and verifying the necessary evidence may be somewhat complex.) Conversely, successfully completing a learning programme will mean nothing in terms of gaining a qualification, unless the required level of competence has also been gained.

This does not mean that those whose business it is to provide learning programmes are now out of a job. It does mean, however, that the volume of their trade will depend on whether they can provide a more cost-effective (or enjoyable) route to competence than an individual can provide from his or her own resources. Clients will not tolerate lack of effectiveness or relevance (as they might have done in the past) simply because their teachers have a controlling influence over the award of qualifications, or because the course is a ritual that has to be gone through in order to gain the qualification.

Apart from their expertise in the design and delivery of learning programmes, colleges and their staff have three other things to 'sell'. These are:

- Opportunities for work-based learning (for example in college restaurants, kitchens, hairdressing salons, training offices and farms). In addition to their obvious value to those who cannot gain access to paid employment, a recent HMI report found that they can provide learners with 'a range of experience wider than that which they might experience in employment'.
- Access to assessment and accreditation procedures. Not all people who wish to have their vocational competence assessed and accredited will wish or be able to do this in conjunction with their current employer. Even though an employer will often need to be involved, colleges may act as 'brokers', and also undertake the time-consuming preparatory work involved in the identification and assessment of prior learning.
- Diagnostic services. By this I mean diagnosis of learning need rather than assessment of present levels of attainment or competence.

It is this last service that could be the most crucial one if we are going to increase the level of competence in our citizens and our workforce, and yet it is often neglected, or confused with assessment of attainment. If colleges could demonstrate their ability to provide this service cost-effectively it could become their distinctive contribution to the promotion of NVQs, and also help them tackle all the other changes I described in my introduction. It is therefore worth dwelling on what is meant (as far as I am concerned in this chapter) by diagnosis, and what the implications are for the organization of colleges if this becomes their key service.

Diagnosis requires:

- the identification of the present level of competence of the client;
- agreement about the level and type of competence being aimed for;
- analysis of what the individual in question needs to learn in order to move from the present level of competence to the target level;
- the design of a programme of activities which will enable this learning to take place.

As far as many college-based full-time courses are concerned, the present situation is that applicants are categorized into three very coarse bands of attainment at entry:

- Less than five passes at the equivalent of 'O' Level;
- Five passes or more at the equivalent of 'O' Level;
- Two passes or more at 'A' Level, or the equivalent.

The college often does not conduct any assessments of its own until the end of the first term. These assessments are therefore designed to test progress on the course, rather than to enable the course to be adapted to the needs of the learners. The approach of giving the same learning programme to people within each of the above 'bands' does not serve their best interests as learners, even if they are all school-leavers. It is a common experience for an individual to find some parts of the course difficult while others are repetitive of previous learning. While 'doing the course' can be equated with 'getting the qualification' this situation might survive.

It is not only the definition of the qualification in terms of units of competence, each with publicly stated elements and performance criteria, which will (healthily) undermine all this. School-leavers will have become used to having their individual progress charted through a curriculum which is not only National but also public. Many more of FE's clients will be adults with substantial life and work experience. The HMI report quoted earlier commented that 'students expressed frustration at the failure to take full account of their previous experience when planning the learning programme'. The reaction of those who see themselves more as experienced workers than students is unlikely to be as mild.

One response is to suggest that modularising the provision would give the necessary flexibility. NVQs will certainly make this more feasible because of their own unit-structure (while not making it obligatory: units of assessment can, of course, also be acquired on integrated courses). NVQs will also ease the task of accrediting prior learning. In fact, this might be better described as 'present competence', and its assessment will be no different whether it occurs before, during or after a course.

However, just because one person 'lacks' the same elements of competence as another does not mean that they need the same learning experiences in other to develop that competence. Even less is it the case that one simply needs to give them more and more practice at that element. If practice really did make perfect then all people doing a job would be equally good at it by the time they retired, if not before.

A fundamental, but likely, error is to take the performance criteria used to assess the competence, and misuse them as learning stages. Everyone should meet the same performance criteria, whatever their special learning needs. But we all have these special needs. In order to improve, I may need to be allowed to make mistakes I can learn from. You may need a carefully structured situation which prevents error and boosts confidence. He may need to practice a particular mechanical technique. She may need to grasp an underlying concept.

Note that here I am not talking about the knowledge and understanding that may underpin a competence, or that may provide evidence that I am competent in a range of situations. This may be the same as that which is preventing an individual from becoming more competent, but is not necessarily so. Psychologists talk about the need for teachers to diagnose 'what learners bring by way of knowledge, understanding, sub-skill and strategy that is of any potential relevant to the competence [they wish to learn].' This refers to their learning competence, not their present level of vocational competence.

Conclusion

To sum up, the special contribution of college staff should be their ability to diagnose learning needs, and then to provide the appropriately flexible opportunities to meet them. I trust that they will also contribute to the assessment of competence as defined by ILBs, but here they will, of course, be working collaboratively with employers and workplace supervisors – and may have to keep learning from them.

Many college staff will respond sympathetically to the notion of making their service more client-centred, but will ask how this can be done while at the same time there is pressure to make the whole service more cost-effective. My thesis is that more resources and time spent on initial diagnosis will reduce the amount that needs to be spent on teaching. Indeed, taken to the occasional extreme, it may be that once learners clearly understand the nature of the learning problem and how it can be overcome, they can undertake the necessary action themselves. Not all visits to the general practitioner result in a 'course' of treatment.

I would contend that the problem is not so much one of resources, as one of structures and style. Colleges are often organized as teaching rather than learning institutions, with enrolment procedures designed to get participants on to a course as soon as possible. This is the equivalent of the doctor who gets out the prescription pad as you walk into the surgery.

Some colleges already run part of their provision in the form of learning workshops, within which learners can work at their own pace and level on individual learning assignments, but under the guidance of a tutor. Examples exist in numeracy and language, on the one hand, and for engineering and bricklaying, on the other. These not only emphasize the diagnostic and coaching skills of the staff (rather than their ability to present or demonstrate), they also require a physical reorganization and the design and production of learning materials.

As well as the learning workshop being larger than classrooms and differently laid out, the way they are timetabled needs to change. Individuals may book in to them, rather than a central timetable allocating rooms to classes. Student attendance and progress records also need to change. The recording of achievement becomes central: it both provides an on-going diagnostic service for learners, and monitors their progress and the adequacy of what the college offers. The computerization and merging of student records and college management systems becomes essential.

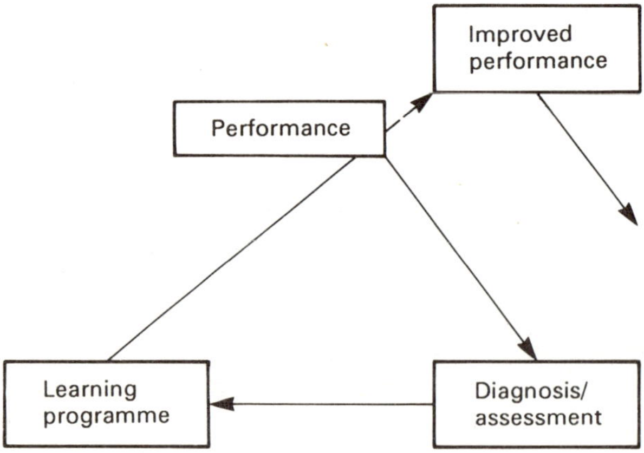

Figure 11.1 *The new approach*

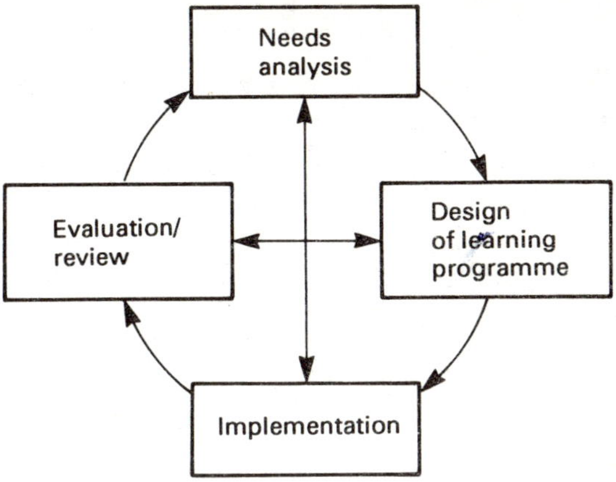

Figure 11.2 *The processes of curriculum development*

The term 'average class size' becomes less useful, and the approach to resourcing which equates 'teaching hours' to 'learning hours' becomes positively dangerous. Recruitment and the associated diagnosis have to become a college-wide function, rather than being delegated to departments or even to course tutors.

Figure 11.1 has been put forward by the FEU as a means of describing the new approach. Although the diagram is simple, as will be seen from what was said above, the nature of the required changes is fundamental. While many parts of many colleges will continue much as before for some time yet, I believe that examining this model of a possible future is both useful in planning for change and in providing reassurance that it is possible not only to cope with all the external pressures but to make better the more flexible provision while doing so.

Resistance is often expressed not because the required developments are difficult to manage (which they are), but because they appear to threaten the position of the teacher and the teaching institution. Here I find another FEU diagram helpful. This is a simplified version of the Unit's well-known model showing the processes of curriculum development (see Figure 11.2).

In effect, what I have been suggesting is that the emphasis needs to shift away from the third (implementary) process, and towards the other three. Good teaching will more clearly be related to the ability to diagnose need, to design appropriate experiences and to evaluate success than to the ability to perform well in front of a class. Perhaps it always has done. Let us hope that the relevant Lead Industry Body takes note!

12 NVQs: Delivering Quality with a Flexible Modular Approach

Barbara Aitken, David Lilley and Sharron Wardman-Browne

The enterprise culture is, along with its impact in so many aspects of business life, triggering some radical thinking about the relevance and outcomes of vocational education and training: from that achieved 'in-house' at the workplace through to the formal processes of professional qualifications to be found in the course portfolios of the main providers (the polytechnics and colleges). One of the most important change agents is the National Council for Vocational Qualifications which has done much to encourage the emphasis on job performance-related outcomes to the vocational education and training process. Through the device of accrediting only those national qualifications which share this objective in their own curriculum design strategies, it seeks to enhance the acquisition on the part of the individual learner of job-related competences: the ability to do the job in the workplace setting.

For all providers of vocational education and training this represents a major challenge, for above all else it will change radically the perceptions and demands of the clients: the learner and his or her employer. We know from the part of our own personal career development associated with the attainment of a professional qualification, if that has been our experience, that until now the process in most instances has been primarily a question of acquiring and applying knowledge: certainly not unimportant, but hardly a complete package of job preparation in itself. Through the work of the NCVQ, we are seeing a change in emphasis. The challenges described here are, of course, primarily faced by the professional institutions and validating bodies who shape the vocational qualifications, and most of the NCVQ dialogue so far has been with them. However, the education and training providers should not sit back and wait for events to arrive at their door. They have a critical contribution to make in balancing work relevance with quality in delivery. All will have to monitor developments as national initiatives evolve, and take further actions as NVQs come on stream.

The NCVQ challenge offers providers the immediate prospect of transforming their 'product' to meet the changing needs of the learner; and the Council has a disarmingly simple message for those involved in providing what they describe as high quality education, training and assessment leading to the award of an NVQ: 'the message is clear: trainees and their employers will look to you to provide what they need, when and where they need it, and in ways which suit them. The key to the effectiveness of your response will be flexibility.' For polytechnics and colleges, who as a group occupy a pre-eminent position among the providers because of their size and traditional near-monopoly in the provision of qualificatory courses, the principal means in conventional wisdom of achieving 'flexibility' is by modularizing the curriculum.

NVQ flexibility through modularization: fact or fantasy?

It is in the convergence of these two strands of thought, as far as 'delivering quality' is concerned, that meeting the needs of the NVQ learner through the provision of modular structured programmes has tended to become inextricably linked. Yet consider a challenging argument. It runs along the lines that the NVQ thrust implies acquiring elements of competence, or small units of skill exercised through effective job performance, which by their nature are highly personalized to the individual learner. The challenge implied in the NCVQ call for flexibility is in making it easy for learners to pick up job-related competence elements where they and their appraisers consider there to be gaps. For the training providers this means just what the NCVQ says: creating flexible opportunities in response to a highly fragmented and complex market demand.

It is here where modularization presents a potential trap if it is perceived as a wholesale and simple way of meeting flexibly the needs of the NVQ-based vocational learner. To many people a module is a structural concept, perceived as a free-standing block of learning comprising a measured input of teaching time which, added to others of probably equal size, accumulates towards the attainment of a qualificatory goal. Or to put another structural gloss on it, modularization means dividing existing course programmes into smaller units of currency from which the learner can pick-and-mix towards the same goal.

Unfortunately for those major providers who can see such structural modularization as a panacea to the NVQ challenge, the argument concludes that any form of course structure, including modular approaches with blocks of learning, will not provide flexibility in the form needed. The NVQ challenge is more to do with providing individual learners with the facility to achieve their own mix of competence outcomes, in the context of enhanced skills in job performance, which additionally are transferable in the work setting from one job to another. The achievement of this vocational effectiveness demands a total learning environment where each individual can draw from a range of sources which are appropriate to the learning required, and at a pace which suits. The system is inherently learner-driven, not supplier dictated. Cohesion and discipline derive not from the traditional planned and structured course programme, modular or otherwise, but from systematic assessment through the NCVQ apparatus of competence elements linked to performance criteria, the accrediting of prior achievement, and credit accumulation towards the NVQ qualification through the National Record of Vocational Achievement process.

The challenge to the providers

The challenge to the providers of vocational education and training in the NVQ setting, and particularly the traditional centres of vocational learning, is to make some hard decisions about what it is that they can contribute best. One view is that the polytechnics and colleges have the expertise (conditional upon some necessary retraining of their academic staff) to fulfil a rehoused role as certifiers or assessors of competence through observing and documenting the evidence meeting performance criteria supplied by the learner. The 'Ministry of Transport Test Centre' analogy is a popular, if somewhat radical, concept of a developing role which must surely be at least part of the future scenario. College-based access and assessment centres are emerging as part of the package in NVQ-related quality service delivery.

There is, however, another practical model of delivery in the NVQ environment where the colleges can shape as well as test the competences. It is a promising role in that it draws upon expertise where they traditionally possess the track record: managing the learning process. The model is based on the notion that work-related competence has an important and interdependent relationship with two other vital ingredients of learning, namely the acquisition of skills and of underpinning knowledge. An example drawn from the vocational areas of business administration illustrates this. The definition of competence standards in general management is certain to include 'personal effectiveness' and 'sensitivity to the environment' as two critical components. Interpersonal skills such as chairing meetings effectively are a possible component of the first, and underpinning knowledge of the legal, economic and political environment of the firm locally and nationally, is clearly important to the second.

In other words, while the performance criteria identified with the elements of competence in any one NVQ are the only important outcome measure, it will often be the case that the learner will need to go through the process of acquiring related skills (especially where they are complex) and/or underpinning knowledge as a prerequisite to discharging the performance criteria at a sufficient level of competence to satisfy that element of the NVQ. It is in this critical relationship that a wider role for the traditional providers in delivering quality to the NVQ learner has potential.

Towards a college-based flexible NVQ approach

Taking the issues already examined here from the perspective of the colleges and polytechnics, the continuing developing of new NVQs across a wide range of occupational areas, and the concomitant demand for a competence-based curriculum, promotes a systematic evaluation of existing and potential learning opportunities within the institution. As has been argued here, prime consideration must be given to shaping or contributing to a learning environment which facilitates relevant vocational preparation for a diverse population of learners.

Moreover, a high degree of flexibility in provision is central to a system where learners seek to achieve the elements of competence specific to their individual NVQ units. At the same time, however, while faced with this potentially resource-expensive situation, the institution will also be subject to pressures to use those limited resources to maximum effect. The question of resources cannot be divorced from the task of delivering quality. The two go hand in hand, and a modular approach may fulfil both needs: backing the NVQ learner with opportunities for skill development and underpinning knowledge acquisition, while at the same time creating learning groups of a size which are resource effective.

An NVQ-related flexible modular approach

Therefore, where a modular approach encourages open-ended and flexible student learning by offering multiple access points, together with the facility to select and credit accumulate blocks of learning wherein competence outcomes can be tested against NVQ requirements, the relationship between NVQs and the modular curriculum would seem to be one of comfortable unity. The counter argument highlights the tensions between the two learning processes. As already stated, where the interpretation of a module implies rigid blocks of learning or time, the flexible individual learning programme could be undermined. In this context, modularization engenders constraint upon the learner and could only be defended in terms of resource utilization alone: hardly the achievement of 'quality delivery'. Yet the potential waste of resources, arising when several learners simultaneously but separately work towards the same competence within the setting of generic skills and knowledge, suggests that modularization of a different nature would be useful if it can be developed on NVQ terms.

Given that achievement of an NVQ occurs without the barriers or constraints of a traditional course structure, a strategy emerges where the major provider (the college or other training institution) becomes facilitator of opportunities for credit accumulation through competence-based learning. These opportunities become one very important source to the NVQ client in the learner-driven environment. The strategy comprises two modular learning models, delivered alongside the provision of workshop facilities:

- *The NVQ outcome model*
  In this modular approach, small units of learning are identified which target particular NVQ competence elements and performance criteria. The 'module' is defined by the required outcomes to be achieved through the use of specific prepared learning material supported by tutorial and physical resources. On completion of the module, the learner demonstrates understanding and skills in the context of the unit of competence in a suitable way: either by work based real situation performance or if possible by simulation of the conditions in the workshop setting. The module reflects the content of the NVQ unit(s) and is bounded only by outcome. There is a crucial distancing between this approach and the notion of a module which concentrates on teacher input of abstract content over a fixed time period.
- *The generic skills model*
  Reference has already been made to the relationship between competent occupational performance and the acquisition of prerequisite underpinning knowledge and skills. To take clerical occupations as a major illustrative example, there is an evident set of generic skills deriving from that relationship. Written and oral communication, numeracy and problem solving are apparent core skills, coupled with more occupationally specific activities such as word-processing, keyboarding and handling cash. These generic skills have the feature of job transferability in common and can therefore be made available to learners from a diversity of work background. This gives rise to a model of modularization identified in these generic (or core skill) terms and defined by competence achievement at different NVQ performance levels.

Open workshops

To further enhance flexible and wide ranging access for the NVQ learner, and where appropriate to enable competence to be practised, demonstrated, and assessed where modular programmes will not suffice, an open workshop setting is required to complete a quality-contributory environment for NVQ learning activity. In this sense, the open workshop has a separate identity from the generic skills module in that the former offer a learning resource to be tapped by the learner on a selective basis according to individual NVQ competence requirements.

In short, there is a range of NVQ-orientated activities of a workshop or work-related character which cannot be generally described as modular and would be impeded by the potential inflexibility of the prescribed modular approaches. However, by the same measure, there are also circumstances when the workshop setting too is clearly inappropriate, because real work conditions cannot readily be simulated. A significant proportion of general management competences are for instance nearly impossible to demonstrate away from the job itself. In such cases, the assessment of those competences and claims for the accreditation of prior learning and achievement can only be generated from workplace evidence. At this point in time, much work still remains to be done in developing the necessary techniques.

However, obvious examples of the need for and appropriateness of a college-based workshop environment are in craft-based occupational competence areas such as the hairdressing salon and the practice office, both fully resourced with the relevant technology of the day. Ironically, but perhaps not surprisingly, it is in such training territory that the colleges as providers enjoy the longest and most consolidated traditions in vocational preparation.

A case study in delivering an NVQ linked to generic skills modules

It is worth examining the experience of the Suffolk College in developing an NVQ strategy. In this case, the focus has been the London Chamber of Commerce and Industry Business Administration Level 2/3 NVQ linked to generic secretarial and office technology skills modules. With the assistance of external research funding from the Training Agency, and following the dissemination and sharing of findings with other providers, the College has modularized its programmes in typewriting, word-processing, audiotyping and Teeline shorthand into blocks of skills development defined with competence-based outcomes. Commonality with the wider NVQ learning approach is enhanced by the use of locally devised competence statements to link with each module, with the responsibility placed on the learner to manage them in consultation with the tutor or facilitator. In the case of shorthand and typewriting the modules lie in a progressional relationship of three, leading to levels of attainment which also link to Royal Society of Arts examinations. The modules vary in their learning input time according to need, are capable of employing flexible learning techniques, and are timetabled in such a way as to facilitate six standard access points during the year, at present spaced at six-week intervals.

Alongside this flexible access facility, the College has also upgraded an existing training office facility into a realistic learning environment for the effective delivery of the NVQ. The resulting workshop provides the NVQ learner with the means of carrying out realistic office tasks (and real work brought into the office from the wider College environment), to achieve the necessary accreditation of competences. An important factor has been to ensure that the office is sufficiently widely equipped to meet the demands of the NVQ. Essential to that need is an open plan basis including all salient features of the modern electronic office which the learners would otherwise encounter at work. The learner works on an open workshop basis with the tutorial staff essentially fulfilling a facilitating and guiding role: in effect as a further crucial learning resource.

Implications for delivering quality to the learner

Event through partial piloting of these strategies so far, some worthwhile lessons are being gained, predictably based on that critical factor that in an NVQ-friendly curriculum, learning must be defined in terms of outcomes and focused on individual needs. The situation imposes specific demands on the organization, the learner and the tutor.

The obligation on the *organization* is to provide an institution-wide network of workshops; linked to modules with, where appropriate, either specific NVQ competence outcomes, or comprising generic skills and underpinning knowledge. In the design of the learning strategies associated with these modules, attention should be given to opportunities for the learner to acquire, practise and demonstrate competence away from the module, and particularly in the work setting. Close liaison and partnership with employers and other training providers is strongly implied. In the consequent complexity of service delivery, resources must also be invested in sophisticated access units and competence recording systems.

The *learner* is also subject to certain tensions in the NVQ workshop/modular environment. Those who start the NVQ from a traditional learning culture may resist the emphasis on 'students having responsibility for their own progress'. The ability to set and achieve personal targets and to use available resources effectively, may have to be specifically developed in the learner. A part of that support might be the resolving of possible feelings of anxiety, uncertainty and lack of self-esteem. Younger learners especially may lack the ability to take the longer view and may need the support of a tutor (or mentor) who can assist in phasing the NVQ elements of competence to be achieved, so that in particular short-term targets can be identified and met.

As far as the *tutor* is concerned, the starting point is that the NVQ learner is heavily dependent on the move away from traditional teaching methods towards an efficient and realistic system for accessing, and for the accreditation of prior and ongoing development. Yet again, flexibility and adaptability on the part of the tutor is demanded. In particular, he or she must have a commanding knowledge and understanding of the whole programme of the particular NVQ, so that the necessary experiential links can be made where units overlap and can be accredited. As learners within groups will not be addressing the same competencies or performance criteria at the same time, it is essential that careful monitoring procedures are put in place to ensure accurate records of progress.

Much of the tutor's function is exercised in the workshop, where the predominant role is that of facilitator and manager of learning. The careful supervision and guidance involved is particularly demanding on the tutor, who will not have situational control inherent within the traditional teaching relationship. There is no facility or automatic right to decide what, when and how a student is going to learn. The NVQ learning environment clearly requires a degree of tutor ability and willingness to adapt, which obviously cannot always be assured. A proactive and rigorous policy for providing staff development, encouragement and the building of a strong and committed team is a priority.

Recommendations for action in delivering quality

If by 'delivering quality' we mean meeting the learner's real needs (and that has been the underlying assumption here), the pressure is now on for learner-driven, individually tailored programmes within a competence-based curriculum. The overriding characteristic of quality becomes the delivery of small blocks of learning opportunity, provided at a pace and time dictated by the learner. As the NVQ initiative continues to gain momentum, and colleges and polytechnics seek to respond to the requirements of their clients (learners and their employers) for a flexible provision contributing towards the development of occupational competence, the framework of delivery becomes a central issue in delivering quality.

In summary, the framework of an action plan for quality delivery comprises:

- Workshop facilities as a means of assuring opportunities for work-based or work-simulated demonstration of competence;
- An interface between those workshops and an allied structure of modules either bounded by competence outcomes, or focusing on generic skills or underpinning knowledge, to facilitate an environment where NVQ learners can gain access flexibly to activities that are an integral part of gaining and demonstrating competencies in the job or work-simulated setting;
- A thorough process of record keeping, using information technology, to keep an accurate track of the individual learner's progress through the NVQ elements of competence;
- An assessment service for the accreditation of prior learning and achievement;
- A close partnership with employers to ensure smooth liaison between college-based flexible provision and work-based learning in developing competencies;
- A system of access programmes and counselling support for learners as they plan their way through the NVQ route;
- A package of staff development to support teachers in adapting to a new and different role.

In conclusion, colleges and other training providers can contribute qualitatively in meeting changing societal needs. Significant progress remains, of course, dependent on a substantial unity of purpose and co-operation across the whole field of education and training generally. NCVQ are encouraging such a climate, and it should be welcomed eagerly. After all, the challenge to all providers is that they enhance their role as institutions congenial to the real market place; institutions which facilitate the needs of the learner, rather than limit choices.

There is one overriding question to be faced. Who will be the arbiters or definers of valid vocational training in the future? The educational establishment? The professional institutions? The heightened role of the National Council for Vocational Qualifications, and the emergence of the Training and Enterprise Councils present a changing picture. They are likely to continue the argument that, for too long, vocational training has been 'supply-driven'. The development of NVQ-based workshops and flexible modular systems of delivery will put the onus of choice from the menu where it should rightly be – on the individual learner, and his or her employer. That is the meaning of quality.

13 Quality Control and the Management of Institutions

Mantz Yorke

The context

The 'running' on performance indicators has largely been made in the university sector of higher education, where the Jarrett Report's (CVCP, 1985) initial suggestions regarding indicators have been developed further, particularly by a joint working group of the Committee of Vice Chancellors and Principals (CVCP) and the University Grants Council (UGC). Statements by this group (CVCP/UGC 1986, 1987, 1988) show the way in which university-sector thinking has progressed, and it is quickly apparent that emphasis is very strongly on establishing financial data which are implicit measures of efficiency.

At around the same time as the Jarrett study in universities was being conducted, the Further Education Unit (FEU) sponsored a feasibility study *Towards an Educational Audit* (ACFHE 1986). On the basis of a literature survey and about a dozen interviews with prominent persons, this project offered some initial thoughts on what an educational audit might comprise. The follow-up study has now been published (FEU, 1989) which develops the concept of educational audit and suggests a variety of sources of evidence about institutional performance.

A working group of the Committee of Directors of Polytechnics (CDP) reviewed the issue of performance indicators and has suggested the use of six (CDP, 1987), and National Advisory Body Good Management Practice Group (1987) offered sets of indicators for both academic operations and resource management, most of which are statistical in character. What may be of particular interest, as far as student outcomes are concerned, is the Group's listing of educational 'value added' – but it has to be observed that there are considerable methodological difficulties inherent in the development of a performance indicator here.

Work on performance indicators has been taken further in the USA. A relatively recent compilation is Krakower's (1985) list of 410 'measures and indicators of organizational effectiveness'. This seems to be a potpourri of almost anything one might think of, and includes some items which would seem to go well beyond the bounds of practicability (occasionally of legality) and sense – for example, comparing a student's health before and after college [Item 87]; self-report of the effect of college attendance on alumni's personal body care [88]; financial credit rating [98]; percentage voting in elections [128]; and job satisfaction subsequent to college [273]. While Krakower's list does contain some useful ideas, most of which appear to be being considered in the current debate, his blunderbuss approach to the target tends to obliterate the valuable insights.

A more recent survey of the use of performance indicators (Cave et al, 1988) shows that, generally, their state of development is primitive, and that they are very often open to multiple interpretation or 'fudging'. Although clearly many performance indicators exist in institutional management information systems or are available to higher education as a whole, the heart of the educational enterprise – what happens between staff and students – appears rarely in the literature, and is mentioned not at all.

The issue of level

The CVCP/UGC working group identified five characteristics of a sound performance indicator, of which the first two are of concern here in that they require indicators to be, simultaneously, related to the stated objectives of the organization and to be specific, quantifiable and standardized. Standardization is seen as critical to the ability to compare within and between institutions. The problem is that higher education institutions have different missions, whose variance is accentuated once their necessarily generalized statements are examined in operational terms. We are not necessarily comparing like with like.

The potential confusion may be mitigated by disentangling the use of indicators in the management of the higher education system in general from their use *within* institutions. One can press this differentiation further, and consider higher education as a nested set of operations – a bit like those sets of Russian dolls, except that each successively smaller doll has some features different from that next to it. In managerial terms, then, the situation is represented in Figure 13.1 (which would need to be varied to fit particular institutional characteristics).

Figure 13.1 is offered merely as a guide which may help in dealing with the central issue in the use of performance indicators: *Who is reporting what to whom, and for what purpose?* One would expect the answer to vary considerably with the particular operational levels in the accountability network. Figure 13.1 is, of course, incomplete in that it has included

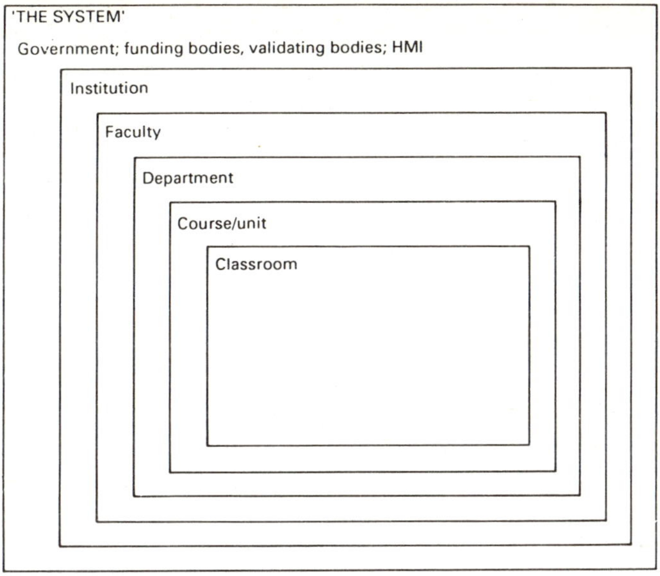

Figure 13.1 *Higher education as a nested set of operations*
Note: 'Unit' will be of increasing significance as credit accumulation schemes develop, and introduces an extra level of methodological complexity.

neither the committee structure dealing with academic standards within the institution (a different link between Course/Unit and Institution which interconnects with Faculty and Department), nor the supporting administrative structure.

At the level of the higher education system as a whole, the government will seem to assure itself that, within resource limits, the number of students has been maximized (and therefore costs per student have been minimized) while quality is kept up to an acceptable level (it may turn out that 'acceptable' is a variable, rather than a constant). In the Polytechnic and Colleges Funding Council (PCFC) sector at least, one can expect to see efforts to enhance access and 'value-added', and a greater attention being given to employment destinations. Mindful of the ministerial approbation given to the polytechnics regarding a marked fall in unit costs, it is nevertheless necessary to make the point that there must be some level below which (high) quality and low price cannot co-exist: one can only stuff so much quality at low prices (to borrow the slogan of a well-known supermarket chain) into the carrier bag before the handles give way and the contents end in the gutter.

The PCFC has clearly articulated its concern with quality, student demand, and price of provision within a set of differentiated programme areas. Although the Council has offered some guidance to institutions regarding the pricing of bids (PCFC, 1989), it is yet to become clear how the problems inherent in the relationshp between quality and price will be resolved.

The Council for National Academic Awards (CNAA) has a rather different perspective on quality assurance and control. In accredited institutions it requires that institutional procedures be demonstrably effective in ensuring that quality exists at (at the minimum) a threshold level of acceptability. In associated institutions, the requirement of quality is monitored in respect of the development and delivery of specific curriculum schemes as well as through the process of institutional review.

It is not my present purpose to explore these issues further, save to note that the requirements of 'the system' typically do not include – save for HMI visits to polytechnics, colleges, and university departments of education – direct contact with teaching and learning activities. It is also worth observing that a number of the terms I have used – for example, quality, value-added and effectiveness of procedures – are not easily susceptible of numerical representation.

But numbers are not without their problems either. When Ronald Reagan was Governor of California he took a dim view of student radicalism at the Berkeley campus of the state university, and cut its funding. The university administrators responded by demonstrating that they were able to educate their students on the straitened budget – but they did not anticipate Reagan's lack of pleasure at an increase in the efficiency with which 'revolutionaries' were being trained (Pfeffer and Salancik, 1978). The moral is obvious: one should not overlook the political implications of performance indicators – the system's view of performance does not necessarily correspond with that of the institution.

The perspective of the institutional manager

My interest in performance indicators is that of a member of the senior management of a large polytechnic, and hence is in the effectiveness and efficiency of its operation. 'Effectiveness' refers, broadly, to the achievement of goals, whereas 'efficiency' deals with the investment of resources in order to achieve the identified goals.

Efficiency in higher education is relative, not absolute, and involves a comparison of outputs with inputs in terms of a difference or ratio (the literature's divergence of view here is unhelpful). The cost per Full Time Equivalent student and the Staff Student Ratio are measures of efficiency which are interpreted through comparisons. However, indicators such as unit costs are not unproblematic: one can imagine an institution reducing its unit costs by accommodating extra students within the original teaching situation, and thereby becoming more efficient. But if by so doing the average performance of the students were to decline, could not the theoretical gain in efficiency be said to have been eroded, possibly to a lower level?

There is no sharp line that divides the constructs of efficiency and effectiveness. The hypothetical example of the previous paragraph, in its concern with student performance, referred to both simultaneously. The efficiency dimension reflected outcome per unit of cost, whereas the effectiveness dimension referred to the extent to which output quality had been developed. Once the criterion becomes 'value for money' it is difficult to decide whether it is a matter of effectiveness or efficiency, or of both. It is possible to have a high quality output at a high cost which would produce an identical ratio to a cheap, low quality output: one *could* argue that both processes were equally efficient and effective despite the clear differences in quality.

In order to resolve the dilemma, one can, of course, look to organizational goals and the extent to which they have been achieved. If the institutional aim is to develop students' abilities to a high level, then a low-cost but modest attainment represents relative ineffectiveness: on the other hand, an institution strongly committed to access for the traditionally disadvantaged might be satisfied with a similar level of student achievement. A persistent difficulty for higher education is that institutional aims are stated at such a high level of generality that they admit of a variety of interpretations of effectiveness and, despite the PCFC's requirement that institutions produce strategic plans, such evidence as is available suggests that these are likely not to give much specific detail regarding targets at sub-institutional levels. A corollary of this situation would be the possible use of performance indicators out of context and for political purposes – which could be in or against the institutional interest.

It is perhaps worth noting a finding from a CNAA-funded project I led, that, of the four institutions involved, only one made specific reference in its mission to its hinterland's structure plan (Yorke, 1990): most higher education institutions acknowledge a regional constituency, and hence might wish to use this aspect of performance as a criterion of effectiveness.

Given an appropriate specification of institutional goals (which, in principle, would not seem to present too much difficulty), it is possible to evaluate the extent to which these have been achieved. One would expect this to be of considerable interest to the two funding councils. The institutional manager needs this evaluation in order to identify:

- where areas of excellence exist (in order to transfer good practice into other parts of the institution);

- where there are particular weaknesses (in order to take corrective action);
- where improvements can be made in those areas that are neither outstandingly good nor outstandingly bad.

To follow these up requires attention to the ways in which the institution operates – to its internal processes. (Funding Councils are likely to be relatively uninterested in how an institution chooses to manage its affairs as long as it delivers acceptable outcomes, but the CNAA has a keen interest in processes impacting on quality assurance and control.) In an earlier paper (Yorke, 1987) I showed how, in assessing institutional performance, one has to bear in mind the variety of feedback relationships that exist among goals and processes. The *dynamics* of effectiveness (for instance, acknowledging that income from research and consultancy is an *outcome* of a year's activity and also an *input* into future activity) have not been well-recognized in the 'effectiveness literature'.

Following Antia (1976) – and, perhaps, catastrophe theory – there is probably a threshold level in each area of institutional functioning below which performance has a deleterious impact on other areas. It is also possible that there is an upper boundary in each area *above* which there is a negative impact. Consider the following, which may be apocryphal but has a certain plausibility. It is said that one university faced with severe cuts by the UGC in 1981 decided to commit its staff to income generation while employing relatively cheap part-time staff to teach its students. While the income-generation was successful, the arrangements for teaching may have had a detrimental effect on student achievement. The lesson for managers from both the literature and anecdote is that one can only *optimize* effectiveness across the various aspects of performance within the general framework of external expectations and constraints.

The CNAA-funded project on effectiveness (Yorke, 1990), to which reference was made earlier, identified a number of instances in the participating institutions where problems with processes had probably had an adverse effect on institutional performance. Table 13.1 indicates some of the problems that surfaced during the project.

A number of the problems identified in Table 13.1 will have had a clear impact on the student experience in the respective institutions, but we should now turn our attention here to the heart of institutional functioning: the relationship between teacher and student. Let us take an indicative example whose general approach can be extended to other areas. If we take staff quality and development as the focus of interest, we have to acknowledge that this is interrelated with other aspects of institutional functioning, notably curricula, student quality and development, and campus climate (see Yorke 1987 for a fuller account). As a

Resource issues

- Under-resourcing of programmes, particularly capital funding. A critical area was that of computing (well known within the PCFC sector, and now undergoing amelioration by the Council's capital allocations).
- The attraction of overseas students without providing an adequate infrastructure in support.
- Resource problems being passed up and beyond the committee responsible for academic standards in the quality control system (because they were beyond its terms of reference), and relatively little remedial action being taken at institutional level.
- The allocation of staff development resources without reference to institutional need.

Structural issues

- Inadequate articulation of an Academic Board's sub-committee structure, resulting in ambiguity and uncertainty regarding the purviews of committees responsible for academic development and academic standards.
- Liability in an institution's managerial structure resulting in a short-circuiting of the decision-making hierarchy.

Dualisms

- An institutional commitment to access while a course asserted a commitment to high entry standards.
- Income-generating short course activity divided between two separate service units with radically different philosophies and separate accountability relationships (one to the senior manager responsible for academic matters, the other following the 'resources' line).

Table 13.1 *Some problems regarding processes which emerged during a study of four institutions* (Yorke, 1990)

manager, it is relatively easy (particularly if staff appraisal is in operation) to identify:

- qualifications and experience (including teaching qualification);
- updating/developmental activities that have been undertaken;
- research contracts, consultancies;
- publications and presentations of various kinds;
- external examinerships;
- higher degree supervision;
- membership of prestigious committees.

And so on. One can, with varying degrees of fuzziness, put numbers to these. They could be used as indicators but, important as they may be, they omit some essential qualitative dimensions in respect of the student experience. Being relatively simple and numerical, they may enter management information systems as proxies for the qualitative.

I would wish to give recognition to characteristics such as the following:

- commitment to students and their development;
- quality of course delivery;
- ability to facilitate students' development;
- enthusiasm for one's subject discipline;
- commitment to curriculum development;
- supportiveness to part-time students.

I would wish to argue that, unless evaluations get closer to these aspects of performance which lie at the less-accessible centre of Figure 13.1, quality control cannot be said to be being undertaken with adequate rigour. This raises some traditionally sensitive issues which most current evaluative processes probably duck.

One can suggest indicators or sources of evidence for the second group of characteristics. The problems managers have to solve here would seem to include:

- finding acceptable methods for determining qualitative characteristics;
- developing a rigorous yet economical way of blending the quantitative with the qualitative.

(The problems exist in the various 'boxes' of Figure 13.1, although the matters at stake may vary. It is important to remember to ask the question, 'Who is reporting what to whom, and for what purpose?')

The further towards the edges of Figure 13.1 one is, the more a third problem comes to the fore:

- how can the data and evaluation from an 'inner' box be validly and reliably handled in a more inclusive box without the same ground being tilled to the same degree of fineness?

My analysis, brief and incomplete as it is, nevertheless suggests that stakeholding in respect of performance indicators is potentially widely spread throughout an institution, and that their use is not a matter for consenting executives and management information system personnel huddled together in private.

References

ACFHE (1986) *Towards an Educational Audit: Feasibility study*. (Report of FEU project RP.304). London: FEU (mimeo)

Antia, J M (1976) Critical success factors in polytechnic performance. *Educational Administration* 5, 14–32

Cave, M, Hanney, S, Kogan, M and Trevett, G (1988) *The Use of Performance Indicators in Higher Education*. London: Jessica Kingsley

CDP (1987) *Report of CDP Working Group on Performance Indicators*. London: CDP (mimeo)

CVCP (1985) *Report of the Steering Committee for Efficiency Studies in Universities* ('The Jarrett Report'). London: CVCP

CVCP/UGC (1986) *Performance Indicators in Universities: A First Statement by a Joint CVCP/UGC Working Group*. London: CVCP

CVCP/UGC (1987) *Performance Indicators in Universities: A Second Statement by the Joint CVCP/UGC Working Group*. London: CVCP

CVCP/UGC (1988) *University Management Statistics and Performance Indicators in the UK*. London: CVCP

FEU (1989) *Towards Educational Audit*. London: FEU

Krakower, J (1985) *Assessing Organizational Effectiveness: Considerations and Procedures*. Boulder, CO: NCHEMS

NAB Good Management Practice Group (1987) *Management for a Purpose*. London: NAB

PCFC (1989) *Recurrent Funding Methodology: Guidance for Institutions* (31 July) London: PCFC

Pfeffer, J and Salancik, G (1978) *The External Control of Organizations*. New York: Harper and Row

Yorke, M (1987) Indicators of institutional achievement: some theoretical and empirical considerations. *Higher Education* 16, 3–20

Yorke, M (1990) *Effectiveness in Higher Education: A Study from the Polytechnic and College Sector in Great Britain*. London: Jessica Kingsley

PART V

Delivering Quality in Vocational Education: The Way Forward

This final Part draws together the major issues facing those with responsibility for expanding vocational education and training into the 1990s and beyond, while maintaining and enhancing quality. Fundamental to this discussion is the recognition that for industry to become competitive and for there to be high-quality services, a significant increase in the numbers of individuals participating in post-16 vocational education is necessary. However, while vocational education is expanded it is critical that the concept of quality is central to the process. This requires that senior managers with institutional responsibilities for educational programmes accept current managerial perspectives on delivering quality and incorporate them into an educational framework. The challenge facing educational providers is to expand provision significantly, while at the same time ensuring that the product not only satisfies customer demand but is in itself of the highest quality. It is recognized that there is not a bottomless resource from which to support education and training; indeed, current government policy is to switch the funding of further and higher education away from the public sector towards the customer benefiting from the process, whether individual or corporate. A further challenge lies in expanding and enhancing the quality of vocational education while controlling a diminishing resource base. The implication of this is that not only has the product of vocational education to be competitive in a market sense, but that educational providers themselves have to develop entrepreneurial strategies so as to resource these developments.

Learning and the learner

What emerges most strongly from the debate on delivering quality is the need to focus more directly on learning and the role played by learners. In one sense this seems strange, in that it could be argued that all forms of education have always put the student at the centre of the educational process. We would argue that this is not the case. The themes we have explored, and the contributions from other authors, lead us to the conclusion that at the heart of delivering quality must be the learner, and this requires a major switch of emphasis in the educational process. Put simply we would argue that unless the educational process empowers learners to own their learning there will remain severe constraints in developing the knowledge and skills base required both nationally and locally to compete successfully in an increasingly competitive world.

Traditionally and historically there have been two approaches to evaluating the impact of the educational process on students. At one step removed from the process but in response to broader external controls, a number of variables best identified in terms of performance indicators have been developed to evaluate vocational education and training. These have been explored in earlier chapters and relate specifically to the extent to which the educational process meets the needs of employers in both the private and public sector. The use of performance indicators place emphasis on output variables in terms of variables such as examination results, employment statistics and unit costing. It is recognized that there has to be external accountability and there is a need to monitor vocational education from the perspective of effectiveness and efficiency within a given resource base. Nevertheless, the use and development of performance indicators do not put the student at the heart of the educational process. As discussed by both Barnett and Bax (see Chapters 3 and 6), this approach is a necessary but not sufficient means of moving towards a sensitive evaluation of quality.

The second external focus on the process of evaluating vocational education and training has been to explore with students the quality of the learning experience. The contributions of Norris and Guri (in Chapters 9 and 10) are illustrative of this approach and are particularly relevant to controlling those variables which are seen to affect the teaching and learning process. Similarly, Hind in presenting his case study (Chapter 8) linking teaching to industrial experience illustrates good practice in this field. There is a view, however, explored by Barnett which argues that this process in itself does not put the student at the heart of the process in that the curriculum and its outcomes are predetermined by those in control of the product rather than by the consumer. What this means in effect is that greater emphasis is given to the practice of teaching than to the nature of learning. In-built in this is the implicit assumption that good teaching leads to learning whereas in practice the converse can also be true. And, where in fact 'bad' teaching still results in beneficial outcomes this can often be explained in terms of 'good' learning whereby the learner has taken responsibility in some way for the learning outcomes and set his or her own targets. This is not to encourage 'bad' teaching but to argue we need to place the onus for learning with the learner while encouraging teachers to facilitate the customer owning the product. This view is based on a recognition that unlike many manufacturing and service industries the product of education is the learner him- or herself.

The implications of putting the learner at the centre of the educational process are best illustrated by the contribution of Hinds (Chapter 5). In her case study she describes the implementation of the innovative Independent Study programme which enables learners to negotiate their own educational experience and outcomes. The basis of this approach is to engage the learner in owning the educational experience and negotiating a learning contract. This enables each individual to develop a programme which he or she has constructed within a broad educational environment. Although the case study presented by Hinds relates specifically to higher education, more recent government initiatives, especially that of the introduction of Training Credits, may be seen as a further step towards encouraging the development of individually negotiated learning contracts. As part of the process of meeting customer specifications the use of learning contracts enables the participant to shape the product.

Customer-led output

A further implication of putting the learner at the heart of the educational process is the switch of emphasis it implies away from the inputs into the educational system to a concern for outputs. Vocational education and training is of value to the extent which its products or outputs are in themselves valued by learners, by prospective employers and external funding agencies. A focus on outputs requires a considerable shift of emphasis for those with responsibility for educational provision and curriculum design. The more traditional approach is to determine in advance the aims and objectives of any programme of study and putting in place appropriate teaching and assessment procedures. This programme is then marketed and made available to client groups who will select from the wide range of programmes on offer. Learners, having selected their programme of study, become part of the process but rarely contribute to the design of the product itself. There is clearly an anomaly here. Given that learners themselves create the products of vocational education and training it is they who should be at the centre of designing the programmes of study rather than selecting from a range of products available on the market.

This emphasis on outcomes is typified by current approaches to the development of work-based competencies. This approach to providing vocational education and training takes as its main emphasis the development of work-based competencies determined by Industry Lead Bodies (ILBs) made up of the appropriate industrial, commercial and professional groups. Learners are encouraged to display competence in the work environment which is then credited towards a formal qualification. There is no doubt that the emphasis of this approach is firmly on measurable outputs. However, the ownership of the product lies clearly with those who have pre-determined the occupational standards and the competencies required to demonstrate the fulfilment of these standards. As such the learner plays a relatively minor role in creating the product. The conceptual switch to emphasizing outputs is important but the failure to include the learner in this movement is likely, we believe, to result in a trained workforce better equipped to deal with the present rather than the future. To adopt an approach that focuses fully on output it is necessary to facilitate the development of innovative and entrepreneurial skills rather than to match the learner to what might be described as a sophisticated 'job description'.

The contributions in this volume from Stanton and from Aitken et al (Chapters 11 and 12) go well beyond this. While they argue that the emphasis on competency as reflected in the development of national Vocational Qualifications leads to an output model, they both illustrate the ways in which educational providers will have to review their provision in order to meet the need of learners. In particular, the curriculum will no longer be in the control of the provider but open in such a way that learners can put together their own programmes of study. This, as Stanton points out, places a responsibility on educational providers to offer diagnostic and assessment services leading to the accreditation of past experience and learning towards a national qualification. The use of diagnostic methods will also result in providers developing more flexible programmes of study in such a way that learners can select from a wide range of opportunities in putting together their own learning experience. In responding to this it is likely that many institutions will develop modular schemes based on a credit accumulation approach which focuses on output rather than input. Hence, it is unlikely that there will be a standard module leading to an agreed credit rating, but a wide range of provision of which all major and sub-components are credit rated. Taken with the emphasis on the needs of the learner, focusing on output rather than input will have a major impact on provision of vocational education and training.

Increasing participation and widening access

Current democratic trends and the implications of the Single European Market (the latter issue being explored more fully in Funnell and Müller, 1991), have led to a consensus view from external government agencies, employers and educational providers, that the 16-plus participation rate in further and higher education must be increased considerably, and access to higher education widened. There is no doubt that the participation rate in the UK is below those of other advanced and advancing industrial nations and that economically it makes sense to enhance the training and qualificatory base of the workforce. Added to this there are recognized and acute skill shortages in a number of areas especially the physical sciences, engineering and modern languages. Added to these economic arguments for expansion are those of 'equity' highlighted in a recent report by Smithers and Robinson (1989). They point out the need specifically in higher education to provide learning opportunities to a much wider range of people at different stages of their lives. In particular, they focus on the traditional access groups including women, those from black and other ethnic minorities and from lower income groups as being prime targets for increasing participation and widening access.

Set against this, however, is the educational system in the UK which still retains its hierarchical and selective approach. The funding bias in favour of universities and those institutions funded by the Polytechnic and Colleges Funding Council is illustrative of this hierarchy, as is the lack of a targeted funding to assist Local Education Authorities in enhancing provision and increasing participation. From the learner perspective there is no automatic entitlement to higher education, and the existing selective provision post-16 is determined by broad strategic input variables rather than by customer-driven output perspectives. The result is that post-16 educational providers offer a wide range of activities but in many cases turn students away or redirect them to other courses on the grounds that it is only economic to train, for example, a selected number of nursery nurses or design students. This absurdity continues in higher education, where not only are students prevented from studying the subject of their choice on the grounds that certain provision is 'full' and therefore not available, but nor are they entitled, having gained the entry qualifications, automatically to progress further. A comparison between the UK and other European countries such as Germany or France highlights this point. In these countries students who attain the necessary entry qualifications are entitled to a place in higher education. Sadly this is not the case in the selective system developed historically in the UK.

Continuing education and training for all those between 16 and 18 has not so far been insisted on in the UK, although such a commitment would be one blanket approach to increasing the participation rate. Instead, there are two parallel developments which may have the same effect over a slightly longer period of time. In Chapter 4 Muir has outlined the current debate taking place regarding the implementation of the teaching of core skills for all those studying beyond the age of 16. Of particular interest here is that in developing what is in effect a core curriculum for those continuing in further and vocational education the boundaries between disciplines become loosened. If students are requiring a set of core transferable skills, whether they study design or nursery nursing may become less important in terms of future employment. In one sense this seems unlikely, but if one recognizes that in many cases the formal study of 'A' levels bears a minimal relationship, not only to degree class but to future occupational choice, a well co-ordinated programme of core skills for those studying beyond the age of 16 could have a much greater impact than many of us currently recognize in broadening the curriculum and moving away from early specialization.

The other important initiative likely to have a major impact is the formation of Training and Enterprise Councils. Bax, in Chapter 6, explores the likely impact of employer-led education and training and the introduction of Training Credits on increasing the post-16 participation rate. The major policy switch here is to place the onus on the learner through awarding him or her a credit which can be cashed in for vocational education training. This is a significant step towards an 'entitlement' model and by being consumer-led may have a much greater impact than a blanket approach towards compulsory education and training.

It will be interesting to see whether this approach is extended to higher education. In such a model a student qualified to enter into higher education would be given a voucher which he or she could cash in at an institution of his or her choice. In the meantime Smithers and Robinson (1989) outline a series of steps which can be taken to increase the demand for higher education without changing the existing entry qualifications. They suggest that it should be possible to encourage more of those who are qualified to apply (although there is the question of whether or not they can be assimilated); to raise the aspirations of younger people so that more come through with appropriate academic qualifications; to develop more fully vocational routes; and to open up higher education to those with no formal qualifications (p 31). They also argue the case for developing links between further and higher education institutions and for high-level work outside the Polytechnic and College systems. Whatever approaches are taken increasing participation and widening access must be a major priority of all those engaged in vocational education and training if the aim of improving the qualificatory base of the workforce is to be attained.

Enhancing provision: the 'value-added' approach

Linked to increasing participation and widening access is the recent debate on the extent to which a notion of value added can be attributed to the education process. The concept of 'value-added' focuses on the relationship between input and output measures. Cave et al (1988) describe it by taking two individuals identical in every sense, one of whom has chosen to undertake further study. The measure of what is value-added is the difference made by the two individuals in their contributions to the welfare of the state, be it economic or social. It has, however, proved very difficult to measure education in these terms due to the wide range of extraneous variables which influence the process. For example, the different salaries paid to different professional groups and their perceived benefits to society are in themselves extremely difficult to untangle. Williams (1990) notes that the simplest measure in comparing graduates and non-graduates is in terms of life-long earnings, although as he points out it is difficult to relate this to the quality of any individual programme or study.

A more promising approach, which has been the subject of a recent report by the Council of National Academic Awards in partnership with the Polytechnic and Colleges Funding Council (CNAA/PCFC, 1990) is to relate student input variables to outputs, more often than not in terms of qualifications. There is clearly a concept of value-added if students without traditional entry qualifications to higher education can obtain the same levels of degree class or professional qualifications as those entering with high 'A' level grades for example. As Williams points out it is the case that: 'Institutions deserve as much credit for recruiting unpromising students and bringing them up to an acceptable level as others do for taking in the ablest students and turning them into national leaders' (p 12).

There is potentially much to be gained by developing sophisticated measures of 'value-addedness'. There is also much to be lost if this focuses only on quantifiable entry qualifications and output variables such as degree class, the professional qualifications attained and future salaries. We have already argued that being explicit in defining quality is recognizing the centrality of the student in the educational process. To really get at the concept of 'value-addedness' it will be necessary to develop sensitive ways in partnership with students to identify the benefits which they accrue from continuing to study and in trying to find sophisticated means of quantifying them. It may well be that students who take ownership of the educational process end up providing a great deal in return, whether or not they gain formal or professional qualifications. This is not to undervalue output measures of this kind but to recognize that to articulate fully a concept of 'value-addedness' it is necessary to go beyond those variables which are readily quantifiable.

Occupational impact

Another way of tackling the 'value-added' approach is to undertake more systematic investigations into the effects a trained and qualified workforce have on the workplace. This approach was highlighted by Bax in Chapter 6 and is based on the argument that it is not sufficient simply to quantify the number of people taking up employment but to develop sensitive measures of the impact they have both in the short term and preferably over a longer period of time. To develop measures of this kind will necessitate considerable research and consultancy both from within employing organizations and external to them. What is of particular interest to the employer is the extent to which the educational system is developing employees with the potential to impact significantly over a given period of time. For research of this kind to be of any value it must be action-orientated and engage employers and employees in exploring how best they can work together. Impact analysis may be a means of helping employers to identify longer-term training needs while helping educational providers to focus more specifically on learners as prospective employees. Studies of this kind will contribute greatly to the quality debate and will serve to inform and enhance future provision.

Core skills in higher education

Linked to the emerging theme of educational outcomes in terms of learner skills is the debate concerning the higher education curriculum. The introduction of the core curriculum for those engaged in compulsory education and the proposed 16 to 19 core skills approach are educational initiatives both of which broaden the curriculum and thereby make it less specialized. This will have an indirect effect on higher education provision in that those studying at this level will in future have a broader educational base on which to build. Consequently, they may have less detailed subject knowledge, which will require the higher education curriculum to be broadened. This could have a major influence on Degree-level provision. In particular it is likely to encourage students to delay their occupational and professional choices more than is the case now. Higher education might well serve to extend the core skills approach and offer selective subject specialism, to be built on at Master's Degree level through work-based projects to develop professional and vocational qualifications. Although speculative, the effects of widening access and increasing participation in higher education must not be underestimated. A philosophy of moving towards mass higher education at the same time changes the nature of the provision, and is likely to tailor it towards the needs of the client group which is becoming broader. The generic skills pertaining to higher education have already been explored by us in this volume and would appear to be in line with what employers and external agencies perceive as the needs of society in providing high quality services and competitive industries.

At the same time there are now emerging selective initiatives aimed specifically at the higher education curriculum. Wright (1990) analyses the impact the 'Enterprise in Higher Education' initiative has had since its inception by the then Manpower Services Commission in late 1987. Higher educational institutions were invited to submit plans to make it possible for their students to develop competencies and attitudes relevant to enterprise. Again, the focus is on developing entrepreneurial skills which enable students to participate in and benefit from the educational process. These aptitudes and competencies were predetermined in terms of being linked to the world of work while recognizing the significant role learners and future employees would play in applying such learning. The extent to which this initiative has been successful as yet remains unknown. However, taken together with the significant changes in broadening the curriculum up to the age of 18, the autonomy of higher educational institutions to develop their own curricula is now a matter for debate. It is our view that the next five years will see the development of a core-skill approach to post-18 programmes of study which focus on developing entrepreneurial skills in learners which are derived less from the discipline base under formal investigation and more from the future economic and social changes resulting from entry into the Single European Market and other structural changes within the European Community.

Institutional aims and goals

It has already been recognized that different educational providers offer differing learning experiences to their client groups. To some extent students themselves select from the range of educational experiences on offer including, for example, studying 'A' Levels in a school environment, moving to a college environment to take either 'A' Levels or more vocationally-orientated courses or to take up employment and study part-time on a day-release basis. Similarly, when choosing higher education possible students select from the different kinds of institutions available and different subjects on offer. However, as an individual progresses through the educational system, opportunities for choice become fewer and selection becomes greater. In recognizing the different roles educational institutions play in terms of developing high quality products it is necessary to focus on the stated aims and goals of the provider. This is often referred to as the 'mission statement' or 'corporate statement of purpose'. The importance of making clear what is on offer and in developing a marketing perspective cannot be over estimated as it determines the criteria by which quality can be judged. As Williams and Loder (1990) point out marketing and quality are strongly linked, it now being more widely recognized that in a competitive market students' perception of the educational experiences offered might well be critical in gaining future and additional resourcing.

In reviewing contemporary approaches to Total Quality Management (TQM) the need for there to be a corporate approach to delivering quality has already been noted. In developing an institutional statement of purpose it is important to include a commitment to quality which is embraced at senior management level. This commitment must lead to a clear policy statement which offers at an operational level strategies for implementation. It is through these strategies that the commitment to quality at a policy level is more likely to lead to an institutional awareness about the need for delivering quality vocational education.

The approaches and techniques offered by the total quality approach are clearly applicable to educational institutions. It is critical to engage all those who have a role to play in the institution in recognizing the value of striving to deliver quality and ensuring that operational practice is in line with the corporate needs of the institution. The importance of open communication has been highlighted by those committed to the quality movement, as has the development of operational procedures to improve quality. There is no doubt in our minds that all educational providers will have to offer a clear mission statement and to demonstrate a concern for quality either through a broad total quality approach or at an operational level by gaining credibility through ISO 9000. Of these it is our view that TQM offers much more to those educational providers offering a wide range of learning experiences. An undue emphasis on operations, as is the case with ISO 9000, in our view limits the impact of putting the student at the heart of the educational process and focusing on output. In many ways the quality of an educational institution is determined by the nature of its product, which places an even greater onus on students themselves to be in tune with the corporate statement of purpose and to participate creatively in the educational process.

Institutional leadership

It was argued in Chapter 1 that by empowering individuals organizations change, although it is through the leadership qualities of individuals that the culture for change is created. This can be seen as a powerful and potentially provocative approach to developing total quality systems. Models of managing institutions based on corporate, and what might be described as over-democratic, approaches have been in vogue for some time. It is only recently that through the Education Reform Act (1988) the legal power of the Academic Boards of institutions including Polytechnics and LEA maintained colleges has been diminished. There is now a move towards an executive style of management at a time when the notion of 'leadership' has been seen to be unfashionable. Consequently there has been relatively little written in the context of education concerning the importance of leaders.

It is our view that leadership is a critical variable in delivering quality. It is also our view that the autocratic approach to leadership is inappropriate but that senior managers and those with institutional responsibilities need to develop leadership qualities which are supportive and facilitative of others. There is, then, the opportunity for leaders to emerge at all levels of an institution by adopting the Corporate Statement of Purpose while ensuring that individuals working with them have the power to make it happen. Leadership is enabling others to work towards long-term goals and seeing through the longer-term implications of institutional change. Within the educational system there is now considerable emphasis on management, which often stresses short-term problem-solving, reinforced by appraisal systems which do not look at the longer-term strategic implications of leadership decisions. Education needs leaders as well as managers. Each individual student should be supported so as to take responsibility for the management of his or her own learning. The responsibility of educational institutions and professionals is to create the environment for that to happen. This demands both our leadership skills and management ability.

Human resource development

There is no doubt that for any organization to be successful in delivering quality it has to invest heavily in its own people. In Chapter 1 a number of approaches to implementing TQM were reviewed, each of which placed considerable emphasis on the need to provide opportunities for staff development, training and advancement. The starting point for such an approach must be to undertake an audit of the skills available within the institution and to put in place through the mission statement corporate aims relating to the future. It is by undertaking a detailed analysis of the skills of the existing workforce in relation to institutional aims that it is possible to work with individuals in developing their skills and attributes. Of critical importance is working through the individual employee rather than imposing institutional objectives on him or her (Müller, 1988). The total quality approach stresses ownership and this implies not only participating in the process but in determining one's own destiny within it. The FEU, the CNAA, the DES, indeed all those external agencies involved in the educational process have made explicit the need to have in place precise strategies for staff development and training. Those institutions investing in themselves are more likely to value individuals taking responsibility for their own education and training and thereby participating more fully in the delivery of quality.

Redefining quality

In Chapter 2 quality was perceived as distinct from but including notions of efficiency and effectiveness. It was suggested that in one sense quality could be seen as a legitimate aspiration of the educational system, whereas effectiveness was measurable in terms of the extent to which quality had been achieved within given financial constraints. Quality from this perspective focuses more on meeting customer needs, whereas effectiveness relates to the extent to which this can be achieved within given external constraints. We think this book contributes to a much clearer understanding of the meaning of quality within an educational context.

The literature reinforces our view that measures of efficiency and effectiveness are not only resource-constrained but in essence are short term. Efficiency relates specifically to the use of given resources within a given time-frame. Many approaches to the measurement of effectiveness do not go beyond the period the student is engaged in formal study other than by the collection of statistical data on work destinations. We would argue that the notion of quality must be defined in terms of the *longer term* impact of vocational education and training on the learner. In this way there is a parallel to the discussion earlier in this Part on the notion of 'value-added'. We think that the longer-term benefits which accrue from vocational education and training are readily encompassed by the notion of 'value-addedness' and contribute significantly towards a more refined definition of quality.

Within this context we would suggest there are five defining criteria contributing to the delivery of quality vocational education:

- Quality focuses specifically on the processes involved in learning and recognizes the centrality of the learner in obtaining successful outcomes;
- As part of this the learner takes ownership of the learning process and through negotiation becomes the major participant;
- The learner takes responsibility for developing and determining the style of delivery of the end product in consultation with the provider;
- A further feature of quality is the extent to which the learner contributes creatively to the ongoing process of learning, having once completed the formal period of study;
- The process empowers the learner to innovate, experiment, reflect and learn from relative failure as well as from success. This challenges the 'zero defect' notion.

We see quality in terms of a value-added approach to delivering vocational education and would argue that the role of educational providers is:

Leading and enhancing educational provision in an efficient and effective manner which ensures that learners fully participate in, and contribute to, the learning process in such a way that they become responsible for creating, delivering and evaluating the product.

Conclusion

Part V has put together a framework for delivering quality and in doing so has attempted to refine existing definitions of the term. In doing so we have identified ten issues all of which contribute in different ways to this process. We represent these diagrammatically here to encourage further debate. Figure V.1 puts the learner at the centre of the process but subsumed within the organization in which the programme of learning is offered. The product is described in terms of output. We have placed arrows going outward from the learner to reinforce the centrality of that position and to focus specifically on the learner's role in developing quality and creating the product. The reputation of the organization and its credibility in meeting statements of quality is seen as being determined by the way in which learners participate in this process and take ownership of it. Similarly, the learner by being in ownership of the output and playing a major role in creating it, is fundamental in terms of delivering quality. We have suggested that there are a number of critical

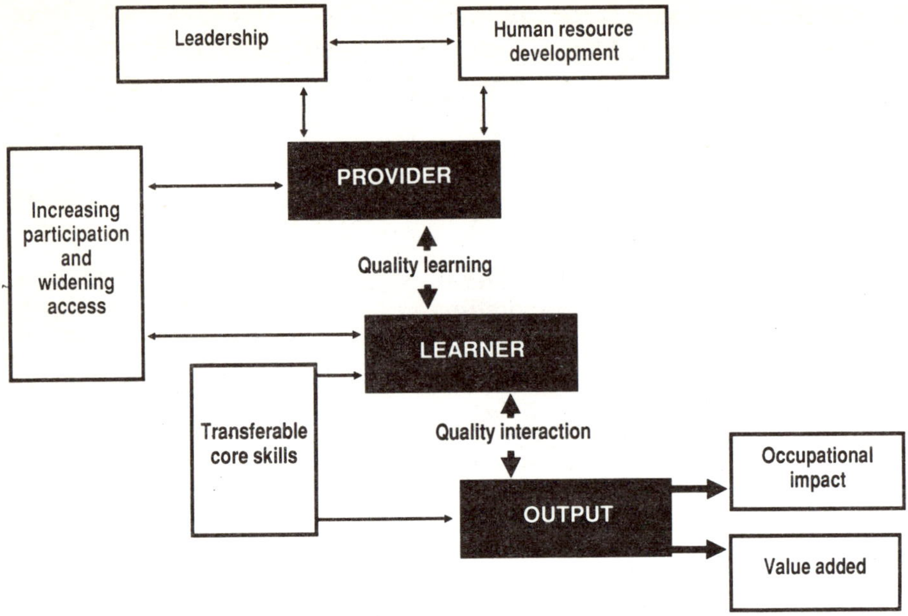

Figure V.1 *The quality process*

issues which are currently influencing the product of vocational education and training.

The debate concerning the core curriculum in higher education may also be a factor in determining output. From the perspective of the organization responsible for providing the learning experiences we have highlighted two factors: the development of leadership, and human resource development. It is our judgement that leadership has an immediate impact on the experiences offered to learners through creating the environment in which they can flourish, and we have suggested this in Figure V.1. The impact of human resource development is on addressing those issues which are in the ownership of education and training providers. There are, of course, more issues than those we have identified but in our view priority should be given to those we have explored in this book.

This book itself has grown through the contemporary contributions included in it. We recognize that the issues we have identified will themselves be replaced in the future by what will then be more immediate and different challenges. As authors and editors of this text we are committed to accepting change, and believe that at the heart of the quality debate is the ability not simply to manage but to create change. This can only be done by putting the student at the heart of the educational process and following through the implications of this. Education and training have a number of customers, some of whom can be seen to be competing. However, at the heart of the process of delivering quality education and training is the role played by the learner in determining, controlling, creating and managing the product.

References

Cave, M, Hanney, S, Kogan, M and Trevett, G (1988) *The Use of Performance Indicators in Higher Education*. London: Jessica Kingsley

CNAA/PCFC (1990) *The Measurement of Value Added in Higher Education*. London: CNAA/PCFC

Funnell, P and Müller, D J (1991) *Vocational Education and the Challenge of Europe*. London: Kogan Page

Müller, D J (1988) Staff development: whose responsibility? *Programmed Learning, Education and Training*, 25, 101–6

Smithers, A and Robinson, P (1989) *Increasing Participation in Higher Education*. London: British Petroleum

Williams, G and Loder, C (1990) The importance of quality and quality assurance. In C P J Loder (Ed) *Quality Assurance and Accountability in Higher Education*. London: Kogan Page and Institute of Education, University of London

Wright, P (1990) Strategic change in the Higher Education curriculum: The example of the Enterprise in Higher Education initiative. In C P J Loder (Ed) *Quality Assurance and Accountability in Higher Education*. London: Kogan Page and Institute of Education, University of London

Index